ALEXIS MONVILLE – MICHAEL DOYLE

I Am a Software Engineer and I Am in Charge

The book that helps increase your impact and satisfaction at work

First published by Six Hands Publishing 2020

First edition

ISBN: 9798627028880

This book was professionally typeset on Reedsy.
Find out more at reedsy.com

Contents

Acknowledgement   v
How is the book structured?   vii

I   The Process

1   Power   3
2   To infinity and beyond   13
3   What do you want?   22
4   What about the rest of the world?   31
5   Grow with your allies   43
6   Fail greatly!   55
7   On your way to a better you   64

II   Part Two

8   Be Impeccable with Your Words   79
9   The Positivity List   82
10 The Five Minute Journal   85
11 Practice Nonviolent Communication   87
12 Moving Motivators   91
13 Ask Better Questions   94
14 The Best Possible Self   98
15 Write Objectives and Key Results (OKRs)   101
16 The Wheel of Life   105
17 The Matrix of Principles   109
18 One-on-one   112
19 How-to I work   116
20 The Four Agreements   119
21 Delegation Poker   123
22 Team Agreements   126
23 Retrospective   130
24 Pomodoro   133
25 Personal Management System   136

About the Authors   140

Acknowledgement

This book would not have been possible without the help of all these wonderful human beings.

John Poelstra, who worked with us on version 2.0 of Alexis's first book *Changing Your Team From The Inside*. This initial working group is what led Alexis to suggest we write *I am a Software Engineer and I am in Charge* together.

All our reviewers who provided straight up, actionable feedback: Dave Airlie, Maria Bracho, Julien Danjou, Marco Grigull, Tim Hildred, Peter Hutterer, Cedric Lecomte, Emilien Macchi, Murray McAllister, Ian Neilsen, Catherine Robson, Preethi Thomas, Vaclav Tunka.

Our legendary open source culture editor: Bryan Behrenshausen.

In addition to the amazing people above,

Alexis would also like to thank:

The family for their ongoing support in my writing, sharing and learning adventures: Isabel, Thomas, Lena, Emma. I love you!

All the friends who I should connect with more often.

All the great people at Red Hat! It is so great to be part of a company where people care and support each other!

Michael would also like to thank:

His family: Terry & Judy, KT & Karl, Steph, Ailsa, Scott, Sophie, and Maya for their lifetime of support and encouragement.

Kathy Waldron for all her walks and talks, video chats, and taking me snowshoeing that one time.

Brad Solomon for demonstrating what turning a passion into a commitment to leadership development looks like.

How is the book structured?

We've designed *I am in Charge* to be a quick, practical book that challenges you to think differently about your ability to impact and influence both yourself and others. We've structured each chapter to help you find insights and try experiments that move you forward by increasing your impact and satisfaction at work.

The book contains an introduction, five chapters, and a conclusion that guide you through a process of changing how you think about yourself, how you work with others, and how you learn through failure.

Each chapter has the following structure:

Why it matters

Here we offer a brief introduction with questions prompting you to examine your current beliefs about the chapter topic. Its purpose is to open your mind to seeing the topic differently.

The story

Here we recount a fictional story following the protagonist, Sandrine, in her new role as Senior Software Engineer (a job she took to escape problems associated with her old role). In each chapter, Sandrine interacts with someone different, and that interaction gets her thinking in a new way, enabling her to take different actions that eventually lead to greater impact and satisfaction in her work.

Sandrine is not perfect. She slips up, promises to change but reverts to old habits, and plans for things to unfold a certain way only to discover they don't play out that way—just like in real life.

What we learn

Here we look at each story's lesson and discuss how it may relate to your own situations. We then ask you, the reader, what you will do with your new knowledge and insights.

Choose one experiment

At the end of each chapter, we offer three experiments for you to try. You can choose to do one or more of them to see what happens when you put yourself in Sandrine's shoes.

Each experiment is structured the same way:

- What is it?
- Why use it?
- Steps
- Further information

All the experiments are located in Part 2 of the book, so you can go back at any time and choose an experiment.

We hope you enjoy what we've created. But even more, we hope the stories and experiments you read and practice here will help you shift your mindset—and increase your impact and satisfaction at work.

I

The Process

1

Power

Why it matters

Recall a time when your words influenced a coworker—a time when someone told you how something you said impacted them, changed the way they thought, or changed the way they behaved. Describe the feeling you had when they shared with you the impact your words had on them.

Now imagine the other person is you.

The story

Sandrine breathes hard as she rushes out of the subway. Her shoe catches the last step and she stumbles, nearly knocking over the elderly gentleman next to her before regaining her balance.

So much is on her mind. Her thoughts swirl. Everything in her new role as Senior Software Engineer would be better, she tells herself, if everyone she worked with were different.

Customers are demanding, changing their minds about what they want from the product again and again. The product manager fails to guide the team by providing them with the focus they need. At the same time, there haven't been enough opportunities to raise this with him, as the technical lead, Maksim, is the only person who has regular meetings with "the PM."

Adding to her woes, she remembers how great her manager, Laseef, was during the interview process. Now it feels like he's too busy to manage the team effectively. Sandrine is only three weeks into the new job and Laseef has already canceled two of their weekly one-on-ones—and at the last minute to boot. The Quality Assurance team are weeks behind in their work and blame the principal software engineer, Alex, for not having finished any of the key features they must test for this release. And all of these are just the things she's aware of.

Sandrine catches her breath. She sighs and feels like she has more to give. But the lack of motivation she felt in her previous job starts creeping up on her.

"I've done my best," she says. "Maybe this isn't the job for me. Maybe I should be in a different company. I just wish everyone around me would do more, be better somehow."

Sandrine is meeting Pranay, a colleague from her previous company, for dinner. She can't wait to tell her what a disaster her new company is and how much needs to change. She smiles as she remembers how Pranay, an executive coach, is able to shift the energy in the room, changing mindsets to get real work done. She knows that venting her frustrations to Pranay will make her feel better.

Sandrine knows the way to Pranay's favorite restaurant. She's relieved to know she'll be on time. The rhythmic beat of her low-heel shoes starts to calm her as she becomes aware of the sound. She wonders what Pranay will have to say about all that has happened in the last few weeks.

Sandrine notices how heavy the restaurant door feels as she opens it, spotting Pranay at a table for two across the room. Pranay looks back at her with a comforting smile.

As soon as she sits down Sandrine begins her tirade, waving her arms as she unpacks all the frustration she's accumulated in the past month. Pranay listens while Sandrine's face glows red as she recounts the most important aspects mixed with all the little details she can remember. The rant is somewhat unstructured, but Sandrine doesn't care. Getting the words out is more important than choosing the right ones. After one final burst, she catches her breath and begins to calm down. The vent brings her the relief she's looking for. Pranay is a perfect listener for that.

"STOP!"

Sandrine freezes. Did Pranay really just say that? She waits for Pranay to relieve her from the awkward silence that follows the injunction.

Placing her index finger in front of her mouth, Pranay gestures once again for silence. Sandrine is shocked. What did she say to merit such treatment?

Pranay turns her head slightly towards the table next to them. Two women, one in her late 20s and another about 40, are having a conversation. In fact, it's not really a conversation. Now that she's quiet, Sandrine can tell that they're venting about their jobs at their company—how bad the company is, how retrograde the processes are, how badly some of the managers behave. From the outside it seems they're having a good time. They laugh as they trade turns highlighting another "fact" about their workplace.

"How do you think venting will help them?" Pranay asks in a quiet voice.

Sandrine begins to draw a parallel with her own rant. She tries to justify herself, saying, "It definitely relieves the pressure, and it looks like it's helping them feel better."

"Good point," answers Pranay. "They may feel better at the end of dinner. The combination of venting and maybe a little too much red wine provides that sensation of feeling better. But what is really different the next day? Are the processes better? Are the managers or team members any smarter?"

It's a never-ending story. Venting only relieves pressure; it doesn't stop pressure from building up again. Those women can keep having this "helpful" conversation week after week, but for what purpose?

Now, Pranay looks slightly to Sandrine's left side. "Do you see those two other people at that table a bit further away, on your left?" she asks. "The younger man arrived the same time you did."

Sandrine had indeed noticed him. She'd noticed him because she thought he was about to cry when he sat down. She doesn't really know why she thought that. He's having a quiet conversation; Pranay and Sandrine aren't able to hear what he's saying. What they can observe is that he's deeply engaged in it.

Sandrine remarks that the younger man seemed to look a lot better now. What's going on?

Pranay can only guess. "I bet they're not venting," she says. "I bet they're inquiring. They seek first to understand. They are trying to isolate the root cause of the problem and work on it."

"Ha ha! You make it sound like engineering work, Pranay."

"Yes, exactly. It is like engineering work. The field, in this case, is not computer science, but the organization and people's behavior."

Sandrine is curious to think more about this. But for now, she wants concrete help on the problems she mentioned at the beginning of dinner.

"Okay," says Pranay, "What is your first question?"

"It's not really a question. It's more that my colleagues are f****** idiots. They're totally incompetent. This is the problem," blasts Sandrine. Realizing her language, she blushes. Pranay stays quiet, leaving Sandrine craving something to once again break the awkward silence.

"I mean, uh, I mean... How do I deal with dumb people?"

Pranay stays quiet, a Mona Lisa smile on her face. At that stage, Sandrine doesn't know what to do. Her mind is racing.

"Why don't they do their job properly?" scrambles Sandrine in another attempt.

At this point, Pranay asks, "When you say 'properly,' do you mean that they are not providing you with what you need to do your job effectively?"

"That's it! They're not giving me what I need to do my job!"

"How do they know what you need?"

Sandrine pauses. "Hmm, I don't know. I just assumed they did know. Maybe they don't. I guess I could tell them. I guess I could ask them for what I need."

"This is really simple engineering work. What changed?"

"Nothing changed. Well, nothing about the situation changed, only my view of it. At first I blamed them for being stupid, but now I see there is another way, something else I can do."

Pranay asks, "Have you ever had someone tell you, 'Oh, the day you said that thing really impacted me'?"

Sandrine thinks for a moment. "Yes! I love when that happens."

"The words you choose can really influence people," Pranay continues. "Each time you choose to say something, it's an opportunity to influence others. This is a big responsibility. Because of that influence, Miguel Ruiz in his book *The Four Agreements* suggests that you should: 'Be impeccable with your word. Speak with integrity, say only what you mean, and avoid using the word to speak against yourself or to gossip about others.' How could I say that my colleagues are idiots when I want to be impeccable with my words? Is that absolutely true?"

"No, of course not. It's not an absolute truth. It's just the perspective I had at that moment," Sandrine admits. "So does that mean to be impeccable with my words I need to push myself to find the right question to ask just as we did before? Going from 'My colleagues are idiots' to 'How do they know what I need to do my job'?"

"Yes, absolutely!" replies Pranay, excited by how quickly Sandrine grasped the concept. "And there's more. Who else can you influence with your words?"

"I don't know," Sandrine says. "There's nobody else listening to my words." Her pause is shorter this time. "Nobody else but me. Are you suggesting that I can influence myself with my own words?"

"What do you think?" Pranay asks. "Could you influence yourself with your own words? Here's an experiment I would like you to try over the next five days. I would like you to care about your words and be impeccable with them. You'll have to catch yourself each time you use exaggeration, each time you characterize an event with overly negative words. And each time, I would like you to try to find the precise words that fit the situation. Once, you find a way to describe the event fairly, then you can try to ask yourself what you could do to influence the situation."

"OK, I'll give it a try," Sandrine says. "I mean, after all, it couldn't hurt, right?"

Sandrine and Pranay go on to talk about other things over dinner. On her way home, Sandrine reflects more on how venting only makes her feel better for a short while. She remembers times when her behavior only encouraged the people around her to join in, which wasn't particularly helpful in solving the underlying issues.

After a few more minutes of walking, she begins to wonder if the opposite could also be true. If she is impeccable with her words, could she influence the behavior of others to have a productive conversation?

What we learn

Have you ever felt as Sandrine does, that venting relieved pressure but didn't stop it from building up again? Sandrine saw she could improve her situation by moving from making definitive statements about it to asking questions that help her identify the root cause of the problem.

By changing her language, Sandrine was able to influence herself. Her new word choice drove a change in her actions, and her new actions gave her new results.

The next time you feel frustrated, what questions could you ask yourself to open up new pathways for action?

Choose one experiment

Each chapter offers three experiments you can choose to put your learning into practice. All the experiments are gathered in the second part of the book so you can refer to them at any time.

Sandrine is committed to trying Pranay's experiment and attempting to be impeccable with her words. Which experiment will you choose?

Be Impeccable with Your Words
Be Impeccable with Your Words is a practice to uncover the power of your words on yourself and others.

The Positivity List

The Positivity List is an index card on which you write down eight topics you enjoy thinking about. You refer to the cards during the day to experience the positive effect these thoughts have on your mind.

The Five Minute Journal

The Five Minute Journal is a journal created by Alex Ikonn and UJ Ramdas. The book is a best seller with more than 500,000 copies sold. The book provides a format for you to create a gratitude journal.

2

To infinity and beyond

Why it matters

"I don't like what you wrote."

"That's not what I was expecting."

"Just forget it. I'll do it."

Have you ever heard statements like these?

Think about the last time something somebody said to you triggered your emotions. What words did they use? How did those words make you feel? What did you say to yourself about the other person?

The story

It's been a hectic two weeks. Sandrine has been busy preparing her submission for a talk at CloudNativeCon, a conference dedicated to cloud-native technologies. Now she's really happy with what she's preparing to submit, but to make sure it's the best it can be, she sends her abstract to Maksim and asks for his feedback. Maksim is a regular speaker at conferences, including this one. Sandrine expects he'll be impressed with what she has written and give her just a few tips that will add that extra polish to it.

Checking her email on the way to work, Sandrine's eyes widen when she sees a reply from Maksim. She quickly taps on the email to open it. The first words catch her completely off guard: "*NOT COMPELLING!*" blaring in ALL CAPS.

Her blood rushes. "What?" she says to herself. "Who does this guy think he is, talking to me like this?"

Sandrine is crazy mad. Her mind starts to boil over with plans of how she's going to put Maksim in his place.

When Sandrine arrives at the office, the smell of freshly brewed coffee greets her. Joel, the newly appointed scrum master, is in the kitchen. "Morning, Sandrine," he says. "Want some coffee?"

Sandrine is pleased to see him and an idea suddenly pops into her head: "I'll show Joel the email. He'll understand how lame Maksim is."

"Morning, Joel. I'd love some. Thank you," she responds. "Hey, Joel, can I show you something?"

She shows Joel the email and he begins to read it aloud in his soft, bass voice: "'Not compelling.'" Sandrine is surprised that Joel doesn't shout when reading the all-caps text. Instead he continues reading: "'By the way, I'm practicing a new level of directness in my professional and personal life... there it is!'"

Joel pauses as he asks Sandrine, "So, you asked Maksim for some feedback?"

"Yes!" Sandrine replies. "And look how he responded!"

"I've only read the first line, but I can see that he says he's being direct."

"Being direct? More like being an asshole! Who does he think he is to talk to me like this?"

"Like this?"

"Yes, like this. 'NOT COMPELLING!' I was very proud of what I wrote, and he doesn't even care about the time and effort I put into it."

"So let me recap here," Joel says. "You asked Maksim for feedback, and by the time you've read the first two words you're already annoyed by the lack of consideration for your work?"

"Yes! In fact, he goes on to explain why it's not compelling," Sandrine says, showing Joel the rest of the email.

Joel thinks aloud as he reads. "Oh, this is very good," he says. "He's has concisely explained the weaknesses in your abstract. And he has given you all the key points that explain what the selection committee is looking for. This is very, very good. Wow! He has even outlined a new version of the abstract for you. People would pay him a lot of money for that, not that he would accept it. Now I really am impressed."

"Hmm. You mean he doesn't do that for everybody?"

"No, he doesn't," Joel says. "This is something our team has noticed. Maksim tends to ignore a lot of requests for feedback. You can consider yourself among the lucky few that, first, get an answer and, second, get a very good one."

"I didn't see it this way. I asked for feedback and I got it. I should be happy with that."

"Yes. But that doesn't mean that Maksim couldn't learn something about how his direct approach impacted your ability to take on the feedback. When our emotions overwhelm us, this is an important signal to consider. We need to listen to the signal and understand what button was triggered."

"I'm not sure I understand."

"Marshall Rosenberg, the creator of Nonviolent Communication, or NVC, said: 'Every criticism, judgment, diagnosis, and expression of anger is the tragic expression of an unmet need.' A negative emotion could be the signal that our ego is standing up to protect us from an attack. Unfortunately, the initiator of the triggering event probably doesn't know they did that.'"

Sandrine looks puzzled.

"Can I help you unpack it a little?"

"Sure."

"Start by observing with empathy and honesty. State what really happened."

"I sent an email to Maksim to ask for feedback and he answered. The first two words were in caps: 'NOT COMPELLING!'"

"OK. This is your first observation of what happened. What else did you observe?"

"Maksim identified the weakness of the abstract, explained what the selection committee was looking for, and outlined a new version of the abstract," Sandrine continues.

"Great! Once you have a good observation of what happened, then look into yourself to understand what emotions and physical sensations you were experiencing. How did you feel?"

"Easy to answer that question! My mind was boiling. I felt angry—very angry."

"OK. Very good. What are your needs that are not being satisfied? Use empathy and honesty."

"I don't know."

"OK. Tell me about what you thought would happen when you sent your abstract to Maksim for feedback."

"I thought he would acknowledge how much effort I put into it and add some helpful advice that would improve it just that little bit more."

"Interesting," Joel says. "Now back to our previous question: What need was not satisfied?"

"The need for my work to be appreciated. When I read 'NOT COMPELLING,' I felt attacked," Sandrine says. "I felt that my work was not appreciated and that I was not being respected as a member of the team."

"So it starts with the work but then ends up being about how you expect to be treated. Have I got that right?"

"Yes."

"OK," Joel continues. "The lack of respect triggered your reaction?"

"Yes, that's it. Being respectful to others is very important to me."

"And what would be your request to Maksim?"

"I want him to treat me like a valued team member. Hmm. Wait. OK. Based on our conversation, I now see he did," Sandrine says."This is not exactly my request, then. My request is more about the form of the message. Those two words at the beginning of his email were not the right way to get my attention."

"Great! It looks like you have the start of something. Well done," Joel says, looking at his watch. His eyes widen. "Whoa. I've got to run to a meeting. Enjoy your day."

Sandrine just manages to thank Joel as he slips out of the doorway. She reflects for a moment on the conversation. Everything Joel said made so much sense. She definitely misread this situation and breathes a sigh of relief that she bumped into Joel before hitting "reply" to Maksim's email and letting him have it.

"I will reply to Maksim to thank him for his valuable feedback," Sandrine thinks to herself. "But first I'll write down some feedback, using the NVC approach that Joel described, about how those two words at the beginning of his email were not the right way to get my attention. In fact, It might be better if I give the feedback to him face to face."

On the way to her desk, Sandrine realizes that it wasn't just the coffee that gave her a jolt this morning. She begins to reflect on how she was not impeccable with her words, like she committed to being when speaking with Pranay. She begins to recall other times where she allowed fatigue or frustration to let her go back to old thought patterns, like venting, because she felt they would give her the relief she was looking for.

Thinking about it more, she realizes that at those times she ended up feeling worse, not better. She re-commits to the practice of being impeccable with her words understanding that it will take a bit of effort for the change to stick. She feels proud as she suddenly remembers what a mentor once said to her: "Sandrine, success is simply restarting."

What we learn

Has your reaction to feedback ever looked like Sandrine's? Her emotions certainly got the better of her. Letting her thoughts proceed unchecked prohibited her from thinking critically about the message she could *actually* take from the interaction.

Sandrine learned that she needed to try to override her automatic response by separating the "how" from the "what." She needed to focus on what the person was trying to communicate not how they were communicating it.

In Sandrine's case she could separate the 'how' from the 'what' in Maksim's message in the following way:

How: NOT COMPELLING!

What: The selection committee won't be interested because they can't see how you've addressed the key selection criteria.

How will you override your automatic response the next time you find yourself reacting to a message?

Choose one experiment

In the introduction, you saw how Sandrine changed her behavior by changing her words. What did you learn from your experiment? Do you find yourself slipping back into old behaviors like Sandrine?

Sandrine is going to practice Nonviolent Communication as she thinks about how to give feedback to Maksim. Which experiment will you choose?

Practice Nonviolent Communication
Marshall Rosenberg created *Nonviolent Communication* to help improve the quality of our relationships by transforming existing patterns of defensiveness and aggressiveness into compassion and empathy.

Moving Motivators
Moving Motivators is a practice to uncover what motivates your colleagues and yourself.

Ask Better Questions
Ask Better Questions is a practice to push you to ask questions instead of stating your opinion. The practice is meant to help you focus your questions on a specific area that your interlocutor cares about.

3

What do you want?

Why it matters

No doubt you need to set goals where you work—usually as some sort of company-wide process that helps you align your work with what your team, department, and company are trying to achieve.

But what's your purpose of setting goals in this context? Is it to tick a box in an HR process? Maybe it's to create achievable goals that will make you look good in the performance review?

The story

The annual performance review is coming. Laseef asks Sandrine to prepare for the review they will have in two weeks. As Sandrine is still fairly new to the company, she wonders what the whole thing really means.

Laseef explains the procedure: Sandrine needs to prepare her assessment of the key competencies for her role, and to define development goals for the coming year. They will share their perspectives on the assessment and agree on the development goals during the formal review. Then Laseef will update the HR system. They will review how well Sandrine achieved the goals during the formal review next year.

Sandrine's heart sinks. "Procedure, competencies, HR systems—this all feels like ticking a box to comply with an HR process," she thinks. "It doesn't feel like it's about my development. None of it feels personal at all. Oh well. New company, same performance review process."

Sandrine talks to Wan, another engineer on the team, who basically confirms what Sandrine inferred from her conversation with Laseef. Wan explains the way he does it. For his personal development, he picks one thing from the company's list of competencies that he would like to work on and calls that his goal. He then selects a training course he believes will help him improve in this area and calls that his plan. For the goals related to his job, Wan chooses things that are easy to achieve and in line with what he's expected to deliver anyway, so there is very little risk that he'll fail. Laseef and the HR system will be happy with him.

While they're chatting about the goals in the kitchen, Joel pops in.

"That sounds like a good approach if your purpose is to comply with the company's HR system," he says. "But you can choose to look at it in a different way. What would your goals look like if your purpose was to increase your impact and satisfaction?"

Sandrine and Wan look at each other for a moment and then look at Joel like their minds just blew up.

"I'm happy to share my approach to goal setting," Joel continues. "Just schedule some time with me." And with that, he leaves the kitchen, the scent of freshly brewed coffee trailing behind him.

It is more than enough for Sandrine to be interested and, as soon as she gets back to her desk, she schedules 30 minutes with Joel for the next day.

The time of the meeting arrives. Sandrine heads to the meeting room and passes Alex in the corridor. He's wearing his headphones. Sandrine smiles but Alex just walks past as if no one is there.

Sandrine and Joel both enter the meeting room at the same time. Joel explains that he's made a decision to focus his development efforts on the next level of his career. His approach is to set goals not from the viewpoint of his current level, but from the viewpoint of the level above him. This makes it easy for him to understand where he needs to develop himself. He has decided to become recognized as someone who can lead more than one team. For that, he thinks he needs to be able to define the objectives for each team and align them with the objectives of the company. He also believes that *how* he achieves this is just as important to his development as actually achieving it.

"First, I looked for our team goals," Joel explains. "Laseef told me that documenting our team goals was something he was working on but that he wasn't quite there yet. He also told me that he would appreciate any help he could get."

An initial discussion with Laseef had made three areas of focus crystal clear to Joel:

- Increase customer satisfaction
- Reduce delivery and deployment times
- Increase knowledge transfer in the team

Joel then explains that although there weren't many details behind these themes, they were enough to point him in the right direction and get him started.

Once Joel understood those three main areas, he started to think about actions someone could take to really make an impact on them—and how he could measure that impact. He started with "Increase customer satisfaction."

"The first question I ask myself is, 'What actions could result in increased customer satisfaction?' The current situation on our team is far from ideal," Joel explains. "Our bug backlog is way too high because we've been prioritizing new feature development over solving known issues for some time. Reducing the bug backlog to create a more stable product is one way that could increase customer satisfaction."

Joel also noticed something interesting from the customer

feedback in resolved cases. Customers that had two engineers paired on a case left more positive comments about their experience than customers who only had one engineer work on the case. He also noticed that cases with two engineers were resolved faster. Joel got a kick out of seeing this nice side effect of pairing engineers, especially because it was originally driven by the need for more knowledge transfer in the team.

Joel believed that by focusing on two things the team could increase customer satisfaction:

- Reduce the bug backlog each month by 50%
- Pair engineers on every customer case (to increase quality, speed of resolution, and improve knowledge transfer)

"OK," Sandrine comments. "I can see how those things would increase customer satisfaction. But won't you get a lot of pushback from the team on those targets? They seem like a lot of work, especially when the team is already overloaded."

Joel winks at Sandrine. "It all depends on what my objective is," he says.

"What do you mean?"

"If my objective is to get the team to accept these two things, then what I'm doing is negotiating and I will likely have to concede something to get their agreement" Joel says. "But my objective is to be recognized as someone who can lead more than one team. How I lead becomes an important aspect of my goal. Pushback is exactly what I'm looking for. I can engage the team through their disagreement. I can ask for their input and begin to create buy-in."

"But won't you just get a watered-down, easier-to-achieve version of the goals, like how Wan does it?" Sandrine asks.

"This is my challenge," Joel continues. "To focus the team on the spirit of the goal, not the literal words I've used to communicate its spirit. If I do this well, the team will discuss ideas around increasing customer satisfaction. If I do it poorly, they will focus on reducing the targets to make the goal 'achievable.' This is how I will measure my own success."

Sandrine pauses in silence. She is once more reminded of her previous discussion with Joel, about the difference between the "how" and the "what" of a message.

"What do you think, Sandrine? Is it a better approach than just ticking a box in a corporate HR system?"

"Absolutely. It certainly feels more personal. What I like about it is that you're still working with the same impersonal HR system, but you've found a way to make your goals meaningful to you. You've taken charge of your own development."

"Exactly," Joel says. "Now, what are you going to do about your goals?"

"Well, first I'm going to identify my purpose for my goal setting. You see, I actually took this job because I felt I wasn't progressing my career in my previous company. I don't want to be back in that position again, so my purpose is to make sure my goals advance my career. You know, someday I'd like to be a Principal Engineer."

"That's great," Joel says. "Where do you think you need to develop over the next year to get closer to achieving that?"

"More technical expertise, I guess."

"I'm sure more technical expertise never hurts, but tell me about a Principal Engineer you really admire."

"That's easy. I'm a big fan of Katie Ots. She's a functional programmer I met in my previous role."

"What do you like about her?"

"The way she works. She has a lot of technical expertise for sure, but it's not like she's trying to be the expert in every situation. She uses her expertise to lead and grow the people around her. And she's like a mentor in her technical community."

"So it sounds like getting more technical expertise isn't the right objective for you," Joel says. "Instead, it's something more around the leadership and growth of others?"

"Yes. Yes, that's it. If my purpose is to lead and grow others, then I can set goals that allow me to develop in that way. Joel, do you think I could help you define the team goals? I think working with you on this would be a step in the right direction for me. What do you think?"

"That's a great idea. Laseef did say he'd appreciate any help he could get. Besides, with the two of us working together, we can use our collaboration to lead the team by example. I'll let him know we're going to collaborate on it."

On the way back to her desk, Sandrine reflects on her purpose for setting goals. Changing how she approaches the process of setting goals changes her course of action. It changes her goals and definitely impacts her motivation, as she can see how she could have a bigger impact—both on her own development and that of others around her.

She can see how it connects with what Pranay told her about her words and how they influence her actions.

Sandrine is back at her desk and wants to create a good draft of her goals using the Objectives and Key Results method before getting feedback from the other team members. She smiles to herself as she realizes that she is actually excited to set goals for the first time in her career.

What we learn

Have you ever approached your goal setting like Wan? When Sandrine discovered that having a purpose to her goal setting made a difference, she decided to set goals that would help her lead and grow others—goals that would increase her impact and satisfaction.

What's your purpose for setting goals?

Choose one experiment

Sandrine is really starting to grasp the concept of influencing herself with her own words. How are you doing?

There are many frameworks for setting goals. It was great to see that Sandrine didn't get stuck trying to decide which framework to use. She just decided to write her goals using the Objectives and Key Results method. Which experiment will you choose?

The Best Possible Self
The Best Possible Self is an exercise to clarify your goals.

Write Objectives and Key Results (OKRs)
Objectives and Key Results is a goal-setting approach that focuses the attention on the impact you want to have.

The Wheel of Life
The Wheel of Life is a tool that helps you visualize how balanced and satisfactory your life is today.

4

What about the rest of the world?

Why it matters

Have you ever worked on something by yourself for so long that you became afraid to share it—afraid that others would criticize your work, that all the effort you'd invested would be for nothing?

What about the opposite? Have you ever started out not really knowing what you were doing, but asked others for their input from the very beginning?

What was different about how you felt in each situation?

What about your goal setting? Is that something you do in private, only to share it with your manager when it's done?

The story

Sandrine reviews her notes from her goal-setting meeting with Joel. She stares blankly at the three main focus areas:

- Increase customer satisfaction
- Reduce delivery and deployment times
- Increase knowledge transfer in the team

"Hardly inspiring stuff," she thinks to herself.

Sandrine remembers how Joel discussed what would really impact customer satisfaction. She notes that, too:

- Reduce the bug backlog each month by 50%
- Pair engineers on every customer case (to increase quality, speed of resolution, and improve knowledge transfer)

She turns her attention to the second theme on the list: "Reduce delivery and deployment times."

She begins digging into all the ways current deployment times are hurting the team. Because deployment times are long, the team needs a good reason to run regression tests. But when the team launches the test for a bunch of changes, debugging and understanding what caused a failure becomes harder to do.

"If we could reduce the deployment time, we could run the regression tests more frequently, which would save us time debugging," Sandrine thinks to herself. "Hmm, but how do we create a goal that will motivate the team to reduce the deployment time?"

Running regression tests on every change would be the ideal goal, but it doesn't seem realistic at this stage. Perhaps running the test every day could be painful enough for the team to get them focusing on the deployment time. That might push them to review the delivery pipeline.

Sandrine and Joel are developing the team goals asynchronously in an online document. Sandrine drafts the first key result for the delivery and deployment times:

- The team runs automatic regression testing daily by the end of the quarter.

She leaves a comment for Joel—"Thoughts?"—and goes on to her next task.

Joel's phone chimes. It's his calendar notification indicating it's time to work on the team goals. He puts on his headphones and opens the shared document. Quickly scanning the document, he sees the comment from Sandrine and reads the key result she's written. "This is all great," he thinks, "but if we run the regression tests every day, we'll have to understand the issues we find and solve them faster. That's going to be really tough." So he writes his own comment in the document—"Too challenging!"—and gets up to fetch some fresh coffee.

Sandrine checks progress on the document and immediately reads "Too challenging!" Her blood starts to boil.

"Damn it!" she nearly screams. "I thought working with Joel was going to be helpful."

Suddenly, something different happens to her.

"Wait," she says. "I wonder what Joel really means by that. Maybe I could ask him to understand more."

Sandrine's mouth broadens into a smile as she realizes she's caught her thought in the moment and changed it. As a result, she now has a better course of action. She's quietly pleased that she's beginning to implement what she's learning.

"When you say 'Too challenging!' what do you mean by that?" she types in response to Joel's comment.

Joel returns to his desk and takes a sip of fresh coffee. He sees Sandrine's comment and realizes that he'd kept his complete thought in his head instead of sharing it with Sandrine, so he replies with more detail.

"I'm worried about the time we have to make that goal work," he writes. "If we run the tests every day, then we'll need to understand the issues and solve them faster. Here's what I have in mind instead. What are we missing?"

Joel then updates the key result this way:

- Average time to resolution of regression is down by 50% by the end of the quarter.

Sandrine's mind goes numb as she reads Joel's suggestion. She thinks back to her initial thought about the team's goal setting and how uninspiring this all seems. She ponders on her own objective for goal setting—to lead and grow others—and then takes a moment to imagine how her hero, Saron Yitbarek, might create inspiring goals.

Sandrine remembers a comment Saron made on social media. Saron was concerned about the sedentary nature of her lifestyle and wanted to do something about it. So she invited her followers to join her in doing something active for 15 minutes a day and eat and drink something healthy over the course of 30 days. Sandrine likes how that idea was easy to understand, yet it lacked something that motivated her to join in until Saron later talked about doing it because she wanted to feel more energetic. Sandrine begins to think more deeply.

Saron
@saronyitbarek

I wanna do a challenge to be more healthy + active, especially for tech folks since our jobs tend to be pretty sedentary.

Challenge is:

1) do something active for 15 mins
2) eat/drink something healthy

Every day for 30 days. Starts tmrw. Comment if you're in! #HealthyTech30

♡ 686   10:29 PM · Oct 22, 2019   ⓘ

💬 296 people are talking about this   ❯

"Hmm," she thinks, "so the outcome is 'to feel more energetic' and one way to do that is 'to be active for 15 minutes and eat and drink something healthy every day for 30 days.' What outcome are we looking to achieve as a team by reducing the average resolution time by 50%? I guess by doing that we could create enough additional free time to do more interesting work. That would be more motivating to us, and it's still aligned to the team objective of increasing customer satisfaction."

Sandrine modifies the goal:

- Average time to resolution of regression is down by 50% by the end of the quarter so we can reinvest our time in more interesting work.

She sends it back to Joel with a comment: "What do you think about linking our goals to the outcomes we really want as a team as a way to motivate us by connecting our work to the real purpose of the goal?"

Joel reads this comment and his jaw drops.

"Wow! That's really powerful," he responds.

He begins to think of the real purpose behind each of the goals.

- Increase customer satisfaction by building a quality product that we're proud of and that meets their needs.
- Reduce delivery and deployment times to do more interesting and valuable work that sharpens our professional skills.
- Increase knowledge transfer in the team to continuously learn and develop from each other.

"If we do these things, then the upside for us professionally is huge," Joel thinks. "We become more valuable to the company and for future work opportunities. That's motivating to me on a personal level, but we're also delivering value for the company and our customers."

What Joel hasn't realized is that by doing these three things they're also building a better team culture.

Sandrine and Joel continue to collaborate on the goals until they feel they're done. They're really proud of their work and feel it will be a huge success for the team. They can't wait to present the goals to Laseef, so they arrange a meeting with him and include a link to the document.

* * *

"So, Laseef, what do you think of our team goals?" Joel asks when the meeting time finally arrives.

"Oh, yes, let me open the document and take a look now," Laseef says.

Sandrine rolls her eyes.

"Wow! These goals look pretty good," Laseef says. "Well done, you two. By the way, what did Wan say? And how did you get Maksim and Alex to agree to these?"

Sandrine and Joel look at each other, both confused and a bit worried.

Sandrine responds, "Um, well, we haven't shown it to them yet. We thought you'd make your minor adjustments and present it to the team."

"I thought the two of you agreed to work on the team goals?" Laseef asks.

"Yes, that's right," Joel replies.

"Then your work isn't done yet," Laseef explains. "You've only created goals that you *think* are good. Please get input from Wan, Maksim, and Alex, then show me what you've got. OK?"

Sandrine's and Joel's hearts sink. They leave the room devastated. Alex is notoriously difficult to get time with. Maksim will tear their work apart; he never agrees to anything right away and always has some reason it won't work. Despite this, deep down they know Laseef is right. If they want to grow their personal leadership, then they'll need to work more broadly with others, even the "difficult" ones.

Sandrine still wonders whether Laseef's management style is lazy or brilliant.

"Wan will be a pushover," she says, "but how on Earth are we going to get Maksim to agree to this?"

Joel winks at Sandrine.

"Remember what I said last time?" he says. "Pushback is exactly what we want. We can engage him through his disagreement. The obstacle is the way. And besides, I think we need to worry more about Wan and Alex than Maksim."

"How so?"

"Well," Joel continues, "if we work with Maksim, then we'll clearly get his commitment because he'll either be on board or he won't. My concern with Wan is that he'll go along with whatever we present. So how can we be sure Wan is truly committed? And Alex...well, you know Alex."

"Maybe that could be a good indicator to know if I'm on track with my goal—to lead and grow others," Sandrine says. "If Wan genuinely cares about the goal, that would be a sign of growth for him. Looks like we need to talk to Wan just as much as we need to talk to Maksim. I'm less confident with Alex though."

"If we can get Alex to show any interest at all," Joel says, "then that would be a sign that we're on the right track."

"Wait a minute, Joel!"

"What?"

"I think Laseef is right."

"What do you mean?"

"I think we've been looking at this the wrong way," Sandrine explains. "Our objective was to create great team goals, but we interpreted that as meaning we had to *create* them—you and me, by ourselves. By having the team really invest themselves in the goals, we're going to end up with better team goals, even if they are not the goals we thought they should be."

"You're right,"Joel says. "By including them, we'll have something that truly motivates the team. And because of that we're sure to make better progress. This is really awesome."

What we learn

Have you ever been so focused on the work itself that you forgot what your objective was in the first place?

Sandrine and Joel learned that creating team goals that have an impact requires gathering input from the entire team. They discovered that by focussing on the objective of the goal they're able to set more meaningful actions because they take into consideration the perspectives of others.

They realized the objective wasn't to see their ideas implemented; it was to implement the best ideas.

How could your work be better by sharing it with others?

Choose one experiment

Sandrine managed to be impeccable with her word and catch herself in the moment of reacting. She was able to choose a more productive path. Have you caught yourself in the moment yet?

Shhh! She didn't want to mention it, but Sandrine has started working on her *How-to I Work* experiment. Which experiment will you choose?

The Matrix of Principles
The Matrix of Principles is a reflection tool that's useful for capturing how team members understand Deming's 14 Management Principles.

One-on-One

One-on-One is an approach to preparing and driving effective one-on-one meetings with unfamiliar people.

How-to I Work

How-to I Work is a practice that asks you to draft a "how-to" describing the way you work to your coworkers.

5

Grow with your allies

Why it matters

What's your biggest obstacle to working well with others? Difficult people? The person who nods and agrees to everything in the meeting, but then doesn't do the work. Or maybe the person who tears apart every idea you have and tells you how it's been tried—and has failed—before. Maybe the person who withholds information, or the one who sends you on a wild goose chase?

Or maybe it's you?

The story

Sandrine hits "send" on an email to Alex to try and get some time with him to talk about the team goals. She sees Wan returning to his desk and asks him when he might have time to discuss the team's goals with her. Wan's answer is disappointing—but, in a way, predictable.

"Not this week," he says. "I have too much to do already."

"Joel and I only need 15 minutes of your time," Sandrine explains. "We need to present back to Laseef by the end of the week and Laseef asked specifically that we get your input on the team goals."

"Are you kidding me?"

"Really. Laseef asked us specifically to come to see you, Maksim, and Alex."

"OK then," Wan says. "I suppose I can spare 15 minutes after lunch. Is that good enough?"

"That's perfect. I'll send you an invite for 1 p.m."

After that first exchange, Sandrine reflects that the task may be a bit more difficult than expected. She and Joel were anticipating that the problem with Wan would be that he'd go along with whatever they proposed. She wasn't prepared for him not even wanting to meet to discuss the goals in the first place.

"Why are people so difficult?" she thinks.

The time of the meeting comes, and Joel introduces the team goals.

"We defined three goals for the team," he explains. "The

first one is around customer satisfaction. The second, around the deployment and delivery time. And the third is around knowledge transfer in the team."

Joel explains the first objective for the quarter:

- Increase customer satisfaction by building a quality product that we are proud of that meets their needs.
- As measured by:
- Reduce the bug backlog each quarter by 50%
- Pair engineers on every customer case (to increase quality, speed of resolution, and improve knowledge transfer)

"The quarter ends in less than three weeks, so I guess you mean next quarter," Wan says. "But even assuming that timeline, achieving those goals seems impossible to me. Laseef really wants us to do that?"

"Laseef wants your feedback and input first," Sandrine interjects.

Wan speaks slowly and nods his head. "Oh," he says. "That all sounds great."

Sandrine and Joel exchange a quick look. After a short pause, Wan continues.

"Look, my biggest concern is that I don't really know what we should do to reach those goals," Wan explains, "and I fear that the end of the quarter will come fast and we'll all lose our bonuses because of crazy goals."

"Good point, Wan," Joel responds. "I had a conversation with Laseef about the team goals and our quarterly bonus. This is how he sees that working: He wants us to sign off on ambitious goals. These should be 'We choose to go to the moon in this decade' goals. If we reach between 70% and 100% of the goals, Laseef will consider that a huge success. If we reach between 40% and 70%, he'll be happy we made progress. Anything below that, he'd be concerned that we did not invest enough energy to make it work. Anyway, we'll have a monthly review, so we'll be able to adjust if needed. I know that I did not answer your question about your bonus and the team goals, but there's no mechanical link between goal achievement and your bonus. It's not something like, 'The team goal is at 70% so you all get 70% of your bonus.' Laseef told me that he's the manager and he will use the same approach he uses today to evaluate the contribution each individual member makes to the success of the team."

"OK. Sounds good to me," Wan says. "Show me the rest of what you have."

"For the second objective, this is what we have so far," Sandrine says as she shows Wan the next page of their document, which reads:

- Reduce delivery and deployment times to do more interesting and valuable work that sharpens our professional skills.
- As measured by:
- The team runs automatic regression testing daily by the end of the quarter.

- Average time to resolution of regression is down by 50% by the end of the quarter so we can reinvest our time in more interesting work.

"OK. In an ideal world, I'd love to have tests running for every change, as that would give me the information I need to move forward confidently," Wan says. "So I see that as our first step toward that ideal world. I'd have the same concern as before about our ability to do that. The key here is really the deployment time. I am pretty sure that we can improve, but I never felt it was a priority for our product manager."

"Another good point, Wan," Joel says. "Product managers are often highly focused on the features that will make or break a deal. They tend to forget about the other aspects of the experience for customers and other stakeholders that will make the relationships last."

"Absolutely," Sandrine adds. "What we want to achieve with those improvement goals is to be able to come back to Product Management and agree on an approach that balances our investment on feature work and the improvement goals."

"OK," Wan replies. "I'm curious to see if they can understand that. What's next?"

Joel introduces the last point:

- Increase knowledge transfer in the team to continuously learn and develop from each other.
- As measured by:

- No team member has fewer than half the average number of reviews of the team by the end of the quarter
- Fewer than 50 reviews provided by the team are considered meaningless or misleading by the end of the quarter

"I am OK with that," Wan says, "but we need cycles from Maksim and Alex, and they don't have them. I feel the deployment time is still the most important thing we need to work on. I have some ideas on what we should start doing."

"Could you write those ideas in a shared document so that we could start talking about them?" Sandrine asks.

"I can do that."

Joel wraps up. "We're just about out of time for our meeting. I want to thank you for your feedback and input, Wan. This is very helpful."

"A big plus one! Thank you, Wan," says Sandrine.

"Happy to help. Thank you," Wan says as he gets up from his seat.

Sandrine realizes Wan wasn't being difficult after all; she just didn't understand his concern about the goals and the quarterly bonus. She and Joel are now eager to talk with Maksim.

* * *

Back at her desk, Sandrine sees a reply from Alex:

"I don't have time to meet with you. I'm working on an urgent customer request that must ship this week, and I'm the only one on the team who can do it."

She doesn't know how to respond to that, and she doesn't have time to figure it out right now, as she needs to meet with Maksim.

Maksim asked to see the goals document before the meeting and he sent a note back just saying, "You don't get what is important for the team to be successful."

With that initial feedback in hand, Sandrine and Joel wait for Maksim in the meeting room. Sandrine tries hard to ignore the tone of the message and to stay curious about the real content of the feedback. She remembers Pranay's words in a conversation they had that followed the *Be Impeccable with Your Words* experiment: "How was your attempt to use the first of Miguel Ruiz' *Four Agreements*?" She remembers her skepticism in her ability to master the four agreements and the impact they would actually have. The situation at hand is definitely one in which the last three agreements are at play:

- Don't Take Anything Personally,
- Don't Make Assumptions,
- Always Do Your Best.

Maksim enters the room and abruptly asks, "Did you get my feedback?"

Joel answers calmly, with a smile. "Yes," he says. "Thank you very much for taking the time to review the draft of objectives before the meeting. Please tell us more, and let's adjust the goals right away."

Maksim repeats that they don't get what is really important for the team to be successful. He tells them that all their goals are too fluffy and will not help the team.

"Which of the goals do you think we should get rid of first?" Joel asks.

The answer from Maksim is instantaneous. "The third one: *Increase knowledge transfer in the team to continuously learn and develop from each other,*" he says. "We're not here for this. We have a critical problem maintaining the core components of the products. We don't have the right people to understand the complexity of some of the components and all the hard work lies on my and Alex's shoulders. I don't want to waste my time with people that are not self-motivated to learn by themselves. We should get rid of them and hire better people. As an example, Sandrine joined the team only a few months back and she knows probably more about our product than people that we hired before her."

"Look," Sandrine jumps in. "I totally agree with you about the problem of maintaining the core components. And thanks for the compliment. But I can tell you that the way I had to learn about the product—and the amount of effort I had to exert to get there—are probably disproportionate compared to the results. I still feel I only know half of what I should about the product and, as you mentioned, there aren't too many people that can provide effective answers."

Maksim simply nods, so Sandrine continues.

"I also noticed one thing: You and Alex are doing roughly 80% of the code reviews, and some team members are conspicuously missing on the reviewer list," she says. "I think having these people provide meaningful reviews would force them to learn more components of the product than just the ones they maintain. As Senior Engineer, I see part of my role as helping junior engineers grow. As we watch them explore new parts of the product, we'll better understand the product's complexities—because we'll observe the junior engineers struggling with them, just like when I worked on the specific workflow tooling Alex created."

"Your proposal to replace it with an open-source automation tool was a very good one," Maksim interjects. "When we created our specific tooling, there were no real alternatives. And furthermore, we wanted to cover all the possible edge cases, which made it overly complex."

Joel gets the conversation back on track. "Based on your exchange," he says, "I think I see that knowledge transfer *itself* is not the goal. The goal is to improve the maintainability of the product by reducing the complexity of our core components. Knowledge transfer is only a means to get to that."

"Yes," Maksim replies, "and I also see Sandrine's point about growing the junior engineers. I would like to invest more time in doing that, but I feel that being the only one able to perform certain tasks is preventing me from doing it. It's also becoming increasingly difficult for me to move on to new things."

Sandrine reads the now-modified last objective:

- Improve the maintainability of the product by reducing the complexity of its core components
- As measured by:
- No team members have less than half the reviews of another by the end of the quarter (so that we increase knowledge transfer in the team to continuously learn and develop from each other)
- Less than 50 reviews provided by the team are considered meaningless or misleading by the end of the quarter

* * *

Sandrine and Joel are back to discuss the goals with Laseef. Their conversation with Wan and Maksim gave them better goals and information about what they have to cover during their presentation to the rest of the team.

The objectives, they conclude, are really the impact they want to have for the customer, and they're able to measure the progress toward those objectives by tracking key results that are connected with the impact for the team. They also have to make clear what success looks like, how it relates to compensation, and expectations for professional development on the team.

Laseef is very happy with the result and tells them that they'll present to the whole team on Monday. He adds, "You are doing a great job with your development goal on leadership."

"Thanks. But there's one problem," Sandrine adds. "We didn't get any time with Alex due to his workload."

"Oh." Laseef pauses. "Well, we need to keep moving forward. He'll have an opportunity to say his piece on Monday. Anyway, I'm still glad that you took on this challenge. This is exactly the kind of leadership we need on both the individual contributor and manager level. After all, leadership is about finding ways to scale your impact."

On her way back to her desk, Sandrine passes Maksim and wonders if it is the right time to give the feedback on the "NOT COMPELLING" email—especially because he clearly does this type of thing regularly, like when he gave the one-liner feedback on the goals ("You don't get what is important for the team to be successful").

Maybe not this time. Providing unsolicited feedback is touchy. But she promises herself she'll do it eventually.

What we learn

How have you felt when you've needed to have a challenging conversation with a team member? This time, it looks like Sandrine remembered to not take Maksim's comment personally and was able to understand his real concerns.

Sandrine and Joel shifted their approach from getting agreement on the goals to getting productive dialog around the goals. In this way, they were able to dig deeper into the concerns that Wan and Maksim had and create goals that they would both contribute to.

How could you change your approach when working with others to get the best out of them?

Choose one experiment

In this chapter we saw Sandrine practice The Four Agreements. Which experiment will you choose?

The Four Agreements
The Four Agreements is a practice to uncover the power of your words and your thoughts on yourself and others.

Delegation Poker
Delegation Poker is an activity a team can use to clarify the responsibilities of its members and stakeholders.

Team Agreements
Team Agreements is a practice that results in a document formalizing how members of a team agree to work together.

6

Fail greatly!

Why it matters

Think about a major project on which you were involved—one that kicked off with enthusiasm and optimism. How did feelings around the project change as the team found roadblocks and shifted priorities? What was the final result? Did it look and feel anything like you remember from the kick-off? Did it ultimately fail or succeed?

The story

The next few weeks zoom by, and the first monthly review of the new quarter is coming up next week. Sandrine reviews progress on the team's goals. Acknowledging any real progress is difficult, she finds, as the metrics are still close to zero.

She's depressed. This is an obvious failure.

Sandrine wonders what will happen to her. She decides to talk with Joel about the results and the upcoming review. Maybe he has ideas on how to dress them up a little, perhaps buy the team a little more time?

Joel can't even make an effort to appear happy to see her. He looks uncomfortable. Does he know something she doesn't? Has he already discussed her failure to lead with the others?

"Hi, Joel. Can I talk with you about next week's goals review?" Sandrine asks.

"Sure. But first I have something to tell you," Joe responds.

Sandrine thinks that maybe the situation is even worse than she thought—and that she might be looking for a new place to work, fast.

Joel continues, "Alex quit this morning."

The news is a shock. Along with Maksim, Alex is a major contributor to the team. And so many times, he's the only person who knows how some things are supposed to work. Sandrine's mind is running at full speed. If they needed another piece of evidence about her failure to lead and develop people, then this is a major one.

"How did you hear about this?" Sandrine asks.

"Laseef told me as he was leaving for a customer meeting," Joel says.

"Did he say anything else?"

"Not really. But he wants to talk about this with us later today."

Things are going from bad to worse.

Sandrine can see the worry on Joel's face. She and Joel tried to engage the team in the goal-setting process, and it looks like they failed miserably. She feels personally responsible for not trying harder to engage Alex. "Is my job at risk if Laseef sees it as a way to get Alex back on the team?" she worries.

Sandrine and Joel blame Laseef for insisting that each team member sign off on the goals at the end of their presentation. She'd noticed how Alex didn't really look committed when he signed the document, much like that day she passed him in the corridor. She realizes she missed a valuable opportunity to speak up.

"Maybe this was too much pressure to put on the team?" Joel says.

"Well, with Alex quitting, I guess maybe it was," Sandrine responds.

Maksim pops his head into the meeting room.

"Are you working on something, or are you just chatting in here?" he asks.

Sandrine gulps and can feel how hard it is to swallow her own saliva.

"We need to talk," Maksim continues. "Do you have a few minutes?"

Joel asks Maksim a question first: "Have you seen Laseef?"

"I haven't," Maksim responds, "but I was just on the phone to him."

"And?" Sandrine prompts.

"This is why we need to talk," Maksim repeats. "Are you available or not?"

Joel nods. Sandrine does too.

"Good," Maksim says, finally entering the room. "What happened to both of you? Why are you making strange faces?"

"Alex quit," Joel says.

"So?" Maksim says. "There are a lot of irreplaceable people in graveyards, you know. Alex played his hand. This time, he lost."

"What do you mean?" Sandrine asks.

"When Alex isn't happy about something, he goes to Laseef and either threatens to quit or sends him a resignation letter, just like he did today," Maksim explains. "In the past, Laseef would be so worried about having him quit that he'd give Alex whatever he was asking for."

Joel's and Sandrine's jaws drop.

"This time he just accepted his resignation," Maksim continues, "and terminated his employment on the spot. In a way, it is really because of you."

Can two jaws drop more than they are right now?

"Because of us?" Sandrine asks.

"Yep," says Maksim, "because of the changes you brought to the team. Laseef said he could see a new way of working for the team, and that the team could handle losing Alex. This is why we need to talk. We need to accelerate the plan to get the rest of the team up to speed. My proposal would be to work with Sandrine to review all the areas that Alex was maintaining by himself. In doing so, we can define a backlog of things we'll need to do."

"It seems that you are taking the news lightly," Joel observes.

"I'm not," Maksim says. "Losing one contributor as valuable as Alex is a failure, and I know that I share a large part of the responsibility for that failure. The other thing I know is that Alex isn't coming back. So I'm not going to stay here feeling sorry for myself. I'll find ways to make it work. I'd like the two of you to join forces with me so we can really bring the team together and overcome this challenge."

"Why do you say you share such a large degree of responsibility for the failure?" Sandrine asks.

"Because Alex complained about the team goals after he signed off on them," Maksim says, "and the only thing I said to him was, 'Get over it.' I didn't want to waste my time listening to his arguments."

"What were Alex's concerns about the goals?" Joel asks. "He never said anything to me."

"I didn't hear anything either," Sandrine says.

"I'll try to keep it short," Maksim continues, "so I'll probably oversimplify. Human beliefs and behaviors are not necessarily my greatest strength. But I guess you already know that."

Sandrine and Joel share a knowing look.

Maksim goes on. "Alex loved to couple himself to complex parts of the system," he says. "My assumption is that he took pride in being the only one able to fix something. It gave him a certain status on the team. At the same time, it provided him with job security. You cannot remove the only specialist you have on something. At his previous company, Alex saw half the team made redundant. But not the specialists. I have to admit that I had adopted a similar behavior. I was frustrated when new people joined our team saying that they wanted to learn but then didn't take any steps themselves. I tended to ignore them, believing that I was helping them grow by being tough and forcing them to figure it out alone. The result is similar to what Alex was doing. Even though my motivations were different, I was being a gatekeeper of my domain."

Sandrine and Joel stare at Maksim in amazement.

"What made me change my mind is the way Sandrine has supported Wan," Maksim says. "Wan turned from someone who just does his job to someone making a genuine contribution, improving the product deployment time—and he did it in just a few weeks. And Joel, I also noticed how you work with some of the other engineers on their code reviews. Not a high impact yet, but a good starting point. So I realized I had a choice. I could continue being a gatekeeper and possibly end up like Alex, or I could decide to scale my impact and grow the team."

"Thank you for sharing all that," Sandrine says.

"Yes, thank you very much," Joel adds.

Maksim smiles. "OK," he says. "What's our plan? We need to get moving now."

During the next few hours, Sandrine, Joel, and Maksim work out a plan for the coming weeks.

* * *

Back at her desk, Sandrine recognizes that she once again made many assumptions. But at the same time, she can now see the results they achieved by talking with Maksim. Their progress on key results may be zero, but they can explain the progress they are making *as a team*.

She's still thinking about this when Laseef stops by her desk.

"I talked with Maksim on my way back from the customer," he says. "Great job on the plan. Thank you. By the way, I have a few candidates interested in joining our team. I'd like you on the interview panel if that's alright."

"Absolutely," Sandrine says. "What should I look for, specifically?"

"Discuss that with Maksim," Laseef says, already hurrying away. "I've got to run to my next meeting. Thanks."

Sandrine still can't decide if Laseef is a brilliant manager or someone who's just keeping things together. Either way, she's come to realize that it doesn't matter. In every situation, *she's* in charge of her thoughts and actions.

What we learn

Have you ever thought as Sandrine did—that your actions contributed to the team's failure? When she heard the news about Alex, Sandrine's mind raced down a negative track, one that stopped her from seeing actions she could take. Luckily, Maksim saw the warning signs for his career path and wasted no time in taking swift action that would drive the team forward and grow his impact and satisfaction. It's another reminder of the value of seeking diverse perspectives.

How could you use "failure" as just another data point that informs your decision-making and helps you identify actions that move you forward?

Choose one experiment

Sandrine has decided to experiment with a Personal Management System and Joel is on his way to prepare the next Retrospective for the team. Which experiment will you choose?

Retrospective
A *Retrospective* is a specific meeting in which a team reflects on what happened during a period of time (one iteration, one week, one month, one quarter...).

Pomodoro
Pomodoro is an approach to managing time and maintaining focus on the most important tasks. A Pomodoro represents 25 minutes of uninterrupted work.

Personal Management System
The Personal Management System is a way of managing your work from idea to completion. The system is a combination of the Getting Things Done workflow and a Kanban board.

7

On your way to a better you

Why it matters

Sometimes the obstacle isn't others; it's how you view your situation. How do you view your personal and professional development? Is it something concretely defined, something you can achieve—or is it a journey where observing and keeping the course are the measures?

The story

"Zain is supposed to arrive today, right?" Maksim asks Joel in the kitchen.

"Oh yes!" Joel responds. "They'll arrive at 1 p.m. We asked them to delay their arrival because Sandrine, their buddy, is off this morning."

"Good job! You picked up the use of the pronoun really well."

"I'm still working on it," Joel says. "I have to admit that when I saw 'they/them' on the resume, I didn't even know what it meant. But after a search on the web, I got it—and realized the simplest thing I could do was just to be respectful of a person's pronoun choices."

"I am glad he accepted our offer," Maksim adds. "Hmm, sorry. I am glad *they* accepted our offer. I think the interview was one of the best I've had in years. I felt they'd add the new perspective our team needs if it's going to reach the next level."

"Totally agree!"

"How about we go out after work with the team to celebrate their arrival?" Maksim asks.

"Good idea!" Joel says. "I'll work the logistics."

"Thanks! Are you joining the mob programming session this morning?" Maksim asks.

"Yes," says Joel. "I may be a few minutes late because I'll be on a customer call with with Laseef and Darius, the new product manager."

"Good! Then I promise not to embarrass you for showing up late," Maksim says, grinning.

* * *

In the lobby, Sandrine welcomes Zain.

"Hey Zain," she says. "Glad to see you again. We're all eager to have you join the team."

"Thank you for the kind words," Zain says. "I am keen to start."

"Here's the program for today," Sandrine says. "First we'll take a tour of the office so you know where everything is. During the tour, we'll drop by office management for your badge, and then make a second stop at IT to pick up your laptop and your security key."

"OK. Sounds good."

"Then we'll sit together at your desk so I can help you configure your access to each of our systems and describe how we use them," Sandrine explains.

"Oh, cool," says Zain. "I always find the onboarding phase of a new job uncomfortable. Everybody knows everything. They use acronyms to describe what's obvious to them, and I don't even know what questions to ask. I'm glad I have someone to support me."

"I started in the company several months ago, so I understand what you mean," Sandrine says. "After we work through the systems, I'll introduce you to your five challenges for the week. It's something I created to make your onboarding a bit more fun. And finally, the team would like to go out after work to celebrate your arrival. Any questions?"

"Sounds great. Will we have a chance to stop for a coffee at some point?"

"Of course! Our tour includes a stop at the kitchen. Let's start with that!"

Once in the kitchen, Sandrine pours some of the fresh coffee Joel has made into two mugs and hands one to Zain. Zain cups the mug with their hands and gently blows on it. Their eyes begin to dart around the room as they try to take in all the details of their new surroundings.

After a moment Sandrine asks, "How do you like the coffee?"

"Oh. It's OK," Zain says. "You know, I may be a little fussy about coffee. Am I able to bring my own dripper to the office?"

"Yes, of course," Sandrine replies. "Half the equipment in here is Joel's. What kind of coffee do you like?"

"I prefer fruity coffees—typically from Kenya, Ethiopia, or Latin America—with beans that are lightly roasted to preserve aromas," Zain explains. "I then use a Hario V6o dripper to extract a richer and bolder flavor. I'm originally from Kenya, and it's funny that I love Kenyan coffee even though I was too young to drink it when I lived there."

Sandrine and Zain continue their tour, collecting Zain's ID badge, laptop, and security key along the way. Sandrine finishes presenting the five challenges to Zain. The challenges are listed on cards in the "To Do" column of a kanban board close to Zain's desk.

"OK then," Sandrine says as she turns to leave. "I'll pick you up to go out after my meeting. Good luck."

* * *

Later, the team gathers at a favorite after-work meeting place. It's part bar, part cafe, part restaurant, and they like this it because it caters to everyone's needs.

Ding, ding, ding, ding!

Joel stops tapping his glass.

"Team," he says, "there a couple of things I want to celebrate tonight, but first let's welcome Zain to our team."

A round of applause erupts, and Joel continues. "Welcome, Zain! We're happy to have you. I'd also like to give out two team awards tonight."

Joel waves two Oscar-like statuettes made of lego in the company colors.

"As you know," he continues, "earlier in the week I asked you to vote for the best failure, and the most promising participation in achieving the team's goals. I have the results." He waves a yellow envelope in the air. "The award for Best Failure goes to the team that pushed a change to all customers because the selection clause that was supposed to only choose 1% of our customers failed." He continues with a grin, "Apparently, we've invented a new form of A/B testing: A/A testing. Congratulations! But seriously, we now know how to properly test the selection clause. I call that continuous learning."

The team members, a little embarrassed by the mistake, now see the upside of their failure. They know something they hadn't known before.

Joel continues. "The award for the most promising participation in achieving the team goals goes to.... drrrrrrr, pish... Wan!" Wan's eyes beam and cheeks grin as he walks toward Joel to receive his award, high-fiving team members along the way.

"I am really proud of receiving this award," Wan says. "I want to thank you all for your ongoing support, particularly Sandrine who has been a huge inspiration to me. Thank you!"

The conversations continue among the team. Sandrine and Maksim find themselves sitting apart from the group. She sees this as her moment to offer Maksim her feedback.

"Do you remember the abstract for a talk I sent you a while back?" she asks.

"Yep, I remember. Have you been selected?"

"Yes!"

"Congratulations!" Maksim says. "Let me know if you want

some help building the talk."

"Thanks again for your help with the abstract," Sandrine says. "And yes, I will need some help to build the talk. Thank you for the offer. But there's something else I would like to tell you. In fact, I have some feedback to give you that I think will help your communication skills. Would you like to hear it?

"Yes, please," Maksim says.

"Would you like me to give it to you straight, or would you prefer me to dress it up a little?"

Maksim seems a bit taken aback. "Umm, straight please." He steels himself.

"When you replied to my message asking for feedback, you started it by writing 'NOT COMPELLING' in all caps," Sandrine says. "I remember vividly how the anger surged in me when I read those two words, impairing my ability to think. I didn't feel respected, as if I was not a valued team member. Thankfully, I bumped into Joel before reacting in anger and doing something I'd later regret. He helped me see past the first two words of your answer and understand the valuable feedback you provided. I experienced this again when Joel and I met with you to talk about the goals. Your opening sentence was quite terse, but luckily I learned from the first time and focused on the feedback you had to offer. What are your thoughts around this?"

Maksim looks up and to his left. He thinks for a moment before saying, "Actually, I do this on purpose."

Sandrine's eyes widen, but she composes herself to learn more.

"My intention is just to get the person's attention so they really listen to what I have to say. People are so distracted with everything that's going on in the company, I thought that by shocking them at the start they'd stop and take notice," Maksim says. "But it sounds from your feedback like this doesn't work for you, and like it may not work for others—or anyone, in fact."

Sandrine smiles and says, "You know, you're highly respected for your technical expertise. I bet people listen to you because of that reputation alone."

"Thank you for the feedback," Maksim says. "Would you mind telling me me if you see me doing that again? I feel it's become so natural that I'll have trouble catching myself."

"Sure thing. Thanks for hearing me out."

Sandrine and Maksim clink their glasses.

* * *

A few days later, Sandrine is on her way to another dinner with Pranay. Sandrine invited her back to the restaurant where they'd first eaten together. She has a lot to tell her friend.

As she opens the door to the restaurant, she immediately spots Pranay. She also notices that the door somehow feels lighter this time.

71

She starts with the "NOT COMPELLING" story, and explains how great working with Joel, Maksim, Wan, and all the others on the team has been. Maksim, she recounts, has even started a mob programming experiment. The whole team gathers for a 90-minute mob programming session every morning at 10:00. The pace at which they're learning and fixing issues in the product during those sessions has been incredible—albeit a little exhausting.

She tells her about how Wan has grown and how amazing he is.

Pranay interrupts her softly at that stage. "Tell me your role in that change," she says.

"Oh, I didn't do much really," says Sandrine.

"I'm not talking about quantity. I'd really like to know the specifics. What did you do?"

"It started with working on team and personal goals with Joel," Sandrine explains. "During our meeting with Wan, it was obvious he was interested in working on the deployment time."

"Please stop downplaying your contribution," Pranay says. "For example, when you say that 'it was obvious,' it was only obvious because you were actively listening to him. Active listening is an important leadership quality."

Sandrine pauses. "Hmm," she says. "I never thought of it that way. Well, once I noticed that, I helped him formulate his ideas and pick one piece of low-hanging fruit that would have the biggest impact on the team's work. And we continued to iterate from there. But you know, he did all the work by himself. I was just there to support him."

"Your impact is greater than you think you know," Pranay says. "You say 'support,' but what I hear is that you are a great coach and mentor to him."

"When you say it like that, you make me feel like I am actually making progress on my own development goal: to lead and grow others," Sandrine says. "But it hasn't been all great. I recently had a big setback."

"Tell me about it."

"Well, we had a new member join our team, Zain. I'm their buddy in the onboarding process. Given that I'd been onboarded not so long ago, I was eager to make the process better for them. But in the end I failed."

"How so?"

"I wanted to make the process fun, so I designed five challenges for Zain to complete in the first week," Sandrine says. "After the first day, they had already completed four of them! They were disappointed, they said, because the exercises didn't teach them what they thought they needed to learn about the product and the team."

"What did you do then?"

"On day two, I sat with Zain and we redefined a new onboarding backlog based on their needs, not mine," Sandrine explains. "And it worked well. They're doing amazing work on the team. I bet they'll win the next team award."

"So what did you learn?"

"Remember our first dinner, when you made getting curious about others sound like engineering work? Well, what I realized is that I was making a product, 'onboarding,' for a customer, 'Zain,' and I never stopped to ask what the customer needed. Talk about not getting the right product-market fit!" Sandrine laughs. "I guess I learned once again to seek other perspectives, and not imagine for a second that I know what reality looks like when I've only considered my own point of view."

"This is great to hear," Pranay says. "How are you putting that knowledge into practice?"

"Well, every time I have an idea to work on something, I make sure I check how it will affect my objectives and the results I want to reach," Sandrine continues. "Then I review that with at least one other member of the team, sometimes the whole team."

"You were pretty frustrated about your situation the first time we met," Pranay recalls. "On a zero to ten scale, how satisfied are you with your job now?"

"I'd say about an eight," Sandrine says. "There are still things that bug me. Sometimes I regress to old thoughts and habits, but I can see I still have more to learn. If I continue down this path, I'll have more impact. You really helped get me started. Thank you."

"Thank *you*," Pranay insists. "I've also learned a lot from our conversations." She adds with a wink: "And as you say so well, you did all the work!"

Sandrine, smiling, says, "Is that supposed to be funny? Oh! I get it. And, by the way, I brought up the topic of my promotion to Laseef in our one-on-one, and he agreed to work with me on the promotion package for the next round!"

"That's great," says Pranay. "I'm really proud of you. It looks like you've taken charge and made some great progress on increasing your impact and satisfaction."

"And now that I'm getting better at it, I'm looking forward to things becoming easier."

"You know, Sandrine," Pranay says with a wise look in her eye, "personal development doesn't get any easier. It's just that you get stronger."

What we learn

Sandrine saw that the things that seemed like no-brainers for her were actually her strengths in action. She also realized that moments when things didn't go to plan were simply opportunities to learn and try something else.

Has someone ever told you that something you thought was easy was actually your strength? What have those things been, and with whom can you speak to see if it's a strength?

Well, you've read this book for a reason: to take charge of your thoughts and actions, and to increase your impact and satisfaction at work.

Only one question remains: What will you do next?

Choose one experiment

Which experiment will you try next? Is it time to do one over again, or select one that you haven't yet tried?

If you'd like to share your comments or feedback about this book with us, email: authors@iamincharge.club.

II

Part Two

8

Be Impeccable with Your Words

What is it?

Be Impeccable with Your Words is a practice to uncover the power of your words on yourself and others.

Why use it?

Changing the way you speak or the way you think is not difficult but you need to invest a deliberate amount of energy to make it happen. Once you catch yourself with one of your automatic reactions, you can choose to change the way you express yourself. *Be Impeccable with Your Words* is one of the Toltec Agreements crafted by Don Miguel Ruiz: "Speak with integrity. Say only what you mean. Avoid using the word to speak against yourself or to gossip about others. Use the power of your word in the direction of truth and love."

Steps

Create a calendar for the next five days with two checkboxes for each day, one for the morning, one for the evening. Once you complete a session, check the box. Display the calendar where it is visible to you, Alexis keeps his on his desk; Michael prefers to have it next to his bed. You may also want to set reminders on your phone so that you really don't forget about the activity.

Morning:

- Choose an event or part of the day when you are going to be conscious of being impeccable with your words. It could be during a meeting, a casual conversation, or choosing to react differently when someone starts venting or gossiping.
- Tick the box on your calendar.

Evening:

- Reflect on the day and make a note on:
- How well you felt you did (this could be on a 1 to 5 scale or use green, yellow, red).
- What you could do differently tomorrow.
- Tick the box on your calendar.

At the end of the fifth day:

- Look back at your notes on the past five days and evaluate your ratings.
- What do you notice?
- What conversations are more difficult than others?

- What will you try next? The same experiment again, or a different experiment?

Remember, rewiring the brain takes repetition, so it's better to focus on changing one automatic reaction at a time.

Further Information

- The Toltec Agreements, Don Miguel Ruiz.

9

The Positivity List

What is it?

The Positivity List is an index card on which you write down 8 topics you enjoy thinking about. The index card can be made of paper that you can keep near you or virtual notes stored on your phone or computer.

Why use it?

Research on positive thinking demonstrated that thinking of pleasurable events requires effort, and that with a simple aid, you are able to do the task more easily. When you are under pressure, you tend to focus on the worst case scenario and consume all your energy in an infinite loop of negative thoughts. By using the positivity list for 6 minutes, you up-lift your mind, making it easier to deal with the challenge in front of you.

Steps

Select your index card. Make it convenient and easy to access for when you need it.

Write down 8 topics you enjoy thinking about. Those topics could be:

- Past events like a birthday party, a wedding,
- People like a family member, a friend,
- Upcoming events like the upcoming summer, your next vacation,
- Even more detailed scenarios that could be totally made up.

Set a reminder on your calendar for each of the next 5 days at a different time for each day.

- Setting at different time for each day will give you different data points on how the positivity list affects your mindset.

Each time the reminder pops-up, pull out your positivity list, and think about the topics for 6 minutes.

- You can choose to focus on only one of the topics, or review several of them,
- Sometimes it is easy to bring back one topic from memory and relive the joy of the moment, sometimes it is a bit harder, and zapping to the next topic gives another chance of bringing memories to the present.

At the end of the 5 days, reflect on what effect the practice had on you and your behavior.

- How did you feel during the experiment?
- What challenges did you face?
- What did you have to do or believe to be successful?
- What positives can you take away from the experiment?
- How can you apply what you learned from this experiment in your life or the workplace?

Some people find that it's helpful to pull out their *Positivity List* in times of troubles, others use theirs as a way to relax at least once a day. How will you use yours?

Further Information

- With a little help for our thoughts: Making it easier to think for pleasure, Westgate, Wilson, Gilbert.
- Difficulty Staying Optimistic Before a Big Audition? Try Using a "Positivity Cheat Sheet", Noa Kageyama.

10

The Five Minute Journal

What is it?

The Five Minute Journal is a journal created by Alex Ikonn and UJ Ramdas. The book is a best seller with more than 500,000 copies sold. The book gives a format for you to create a gratitude journal.

Why use it?

Sticking to the practice and creating the habit of continuing it over time has proven to increase happiness, improve relationships, and foster optimism. The practice is not the only journaling practice. Benjamin Franklin proposed a journaling practice associated with his book of virtues for example.

Steps

The practice is arranged in two parts, the morning routine, and the night routine.

Morning Routine, just after waking up, answer these three questions:

- **I am grateful for.** List three things that you are grateful for.
- **What would make today great?** List three things that would make today great.
- **Daily affirmation, I am.** Express who you are. An example could be: "I am clear and focused on my goals."

Night Routine, just before going to bed, evaluate your day with these two questions:

- **Three amazing things that happened today.** List the three amazing things that happened today. The idea is to focus on the positive, as we have a natural tendency to do exactly the opposite.
- **How could I have made today even better?** Express the one thing you could have done to make the day better. This part is for reflection and growth.

Further Information

- The Five Minute Journal, Intelligent Change
- Benjamin Franklin's Book of Virtues
- A Companion to Benjamin Franklin's Book of Virtues

11

Practice Nonviolent Communication

What is it?

Marshall Rosenberg created Nonviolent Communication to help improve the quality of our relationships by transforming existing patterns of defensiveness and aggressiveness into compassion and empathy.

The Nonviolent Communication model has four components and two parts.

The four components are:

- Observation
- Feeling
- Needs
- Request

The two parts are:

- Empathy
- Honesty

The outline of the model goes like this:

When I see that_____

I feel _____

because my need for _____ is/is not met.

Would you be willing to _____?

Why use it?

The model supports your introspection and reflection of what is going on in the world around you. By practising Nonviolent Communication, you are more able to nurture the relationships with people around you.

Steps

Remember a time and place where the conversation became really heated. For Alexis It was one reaction in a meeting, something he said, he did not necessarily know why, but he could see on the faces of other people that it was not helping. We will use this as an example for the different steps.

Observation

- Take a step back and observe what happened,
- When I see (hear...)
- *Alexis: When I hear you speaking about the complexity of the work of a team that has no representative in the room, a team I was a member of before...*

Feelings

- Now express how you feel, it can be an emotion or a sensation rather than a thought that is in relation to what you observe.
- ... I feel...
- *Alexis: ... I felt a rush of anger...*

Needs

- Now express what you need or value that cause your feelings.
- ... Because I need...
- *Alexis: ... Because I need people to be respected, I need their work to be respected, I need fairness and equity...*

Requests

- Now you can formulate a request that would improve the relationship, without demanding, a concrete action that you would like to be taken.
- ... Would you be willing to... ?
- *Alexis: ... Would you be willing to invite representatives of that team so they can bring their own perspective on those issues so that we can all learn and improve?*

You can expect that you won't get it right the first time, and that you'll need more than one iteration to make it good. Good being, an observation that is really an observation, a feeling that is really a feeling, and so on...

Working on this with a trusted peer could really help.

Further Information

- Nonviolent Communication: A Language of Life, Marshall B. Rosenberg, Ph.D
- Nonviolent Communication Companion Workbook: A Practical Guide for Individual, Group, or Classroom Study, Lucy Leu. Also the workbook is on issuu.com

12

Moving Motivators

What is it?

Moving Motivators is a practice to uncover what motivates your colleagues and yourself.

Moving motivators is a deck of 10 cards. Each card represents an intrinsic motivation: Curiosity, Acceptance, Power, Relatedness, Goal, Honor, Mastery, Freedom, Order, Status.

Why use it?

The practice helps you to understand different perspectives. Something very important for one person could be futile for another. Accepting that there is no good or bad is part of the game.

Steps

First, download and print the cards from the Management 3.0 website. You can also buy sets of cards if you prefer.

Once you have the cards, play the game alone. This is your training.

Sort the cards from left to right. The most important motivation factor is on the left; the less important is on the right.

Consider a change in your life and how this change affects your motivation factors. Move the card up if it is a positive effect and down if it is a negative effect.

You can try with different changes like:

- Change job,
- Change company,
- Buy a car,
- Learn to play a musical instrument,
- Move to another city or country,
- Meet old friends, make new ones, and so on.

Consider the transformation you would like your team to commit to and look at how it affects your motivators.

Bonus: Use the power of the game and play it with your team. Discuss what motivators are least or most important to each team member, and how they are affected by changes.

Further Information

- More about the Moving Motivators practices on the Management 3.0 website
- Moving Motivators is the assignment from the third chapter of Changing Your Team From The Inside

13

Ask Better Questions

What is it?

Ask Better Questions is a practice to push you to ask questions instead of stating your opinion. The practice helps you focus your questions on a specific area that your interlocutor cares about.

Why use it?

We tend to want to solve problems, even when we know that it is much better to help people to find their own solutions. Alexis has received several questions about the need to listen, and the need to ask better questions. Looking for a simple way to explain how it works, he used the GROW model developed by Graham Alexander.

Steps

GROW stands for Goal setting, Reality, Options, Way forward. Let's examine a few examples of questions you could ask for each step in a future conversation.

Be careful not to make the questions sound like a judgment call. The goal is to explore what are the real goals of a person for the current conversation, or for a more long term time frame, and then ask question to help them find their own solution to get there. The questions could also be used in a group setting situation. In both cases, you need to first get permission from the person or the group to provide your help.

Goal setting, what the person wants to achieve:

- What does success look like?
- What would need to happen for you to walk away feeling that this time was well spent?
- What would be a milestone on the way?
- If you had a magic wand, what would you change?
- How much personal control or influence do you have over your goal?
- How will you measure it? (the goal is not the measure, just to foster the conversation and to check that you have the same understanding of the goal.)

Reality, assess the reality (and the awareness of the person that reality is a very subjective thing):

- What is happening now?

- You will need to use descriptor questions to help the person to think more precisely about the situation: Tell me more about, help me understand, I am curious about, could you describe further...
- How do you know that this is really happening?
- What other factors are relevant?
- How do the other stakeholders perceived the situation?
- What are the results of your previous actions?

Options and Obstacles, explore the different options possible to get the desired results, and examine the obstacles that prevent to get the results:

- What could you do to change the situation?
- What have you done or see others do in similar situations?
- What are the options for action?
- What are the benefits and costs of your different options?
- What are the external and internal factors that could prevent you in taking actions?
- What will you do to eliminate these external and internal factors?

Way forward, is when we convert options into actions:

- What option will you choose?
- What will you do and when?
- What support do you need and from whom?
- How will you get that support?

After each conversation, take some time to reflect on what happened during the experiment:

- How did you feel during the experiment?
- What challenges did you face?
- What did you have to do or believe to be successful?
- What positives can you take away from the experiment?
- How can you apply what you learned in your life or the workplace?

Note that the questions above are all open questions; what, where, when, who, and how. This gives the person you are questioning freedom to respond. You might also notice that there are no "why" questions; "why" questions can cause the person you are questioning to defend their actions. Stick to open questions for maximum impact.

Further Information

- The GROW model developed by Graham Alexander.

14

The Best Possible Self

What is it?

The Best Possible Self is an exercise to clarify your goals.

Why use it?

Research shows that building optimism about the future motivates you to work toward that desired future.

Steps

First prepare a visible calendar with five checkboxes representing the next five days. For each day that you accomplish the assignment, tick a box.

Each day, take a moment to imagine your life in the future.

- What is the best possible life you can envision?

- In all the different areas of your life, professional or personal, what will happen in your best possible future?

Write for at least five minutes, use the hot pen technique. Write what comes to your mind without editing (you can write longer if there is a lot of information coming to mind).

Be very specific in your write-up

- Describe a better future in which you are your best possible self, and what needs to change in your current situation, what you will learn, what habits you will change.

You will start the next day with a blank page.

After five days, you may be tempted to continue the exercise because you feel that you can learn more from it. Please do and drop us a note to tell us what was the right duration for you.

Some people find it useful to let a few days pass before reviewing their writings, when you are ready, review your writing:

- Are they different from day to day?
- Do you see key themes coming back over the days?
- Can you write down the themes in the present tense?

One last word, if you miss a day, don't be harsh on yourself. Guilt has a negative effect on our willpower. Success is simply restarting.

Further Information

- The Best Possible Self, Laura A. King, Ph.D., University of Missouri, Jeffrey Huffman, M.D., Harvard Medical School, Massachusetts General Hospital,
- How to increase and sustain positive emotion: The effects of expressing gratitude and visualizing best possible selves, Kennon M. Sheldon & Sonja Lyubomirsky

15

Write Objectives and Key Results (OKRs)

What is it?

Objectives and Key Results is a goal-setting approach that focuses attention on the impact you want to have. The impact is characterized by a behavioral change that the people involved will adopt so that you can reach your objectives and fulfill your aspirational vision.

Why use it?

Reaching aspirational goals takes time. It requires measured, smaller steps along the way to help reach them. The "Progress Principle" is a positive force motivating an individual, a team, or an entire organization to do their best. Achieving measurable steps makes feedback relevant, and further fuels your momentum to realize the vision.

Steps

What is your vision?

- The vision is the dream. The vision is very ambitious and audacious, focused on what success looks like in the near future (3, 5 years, or longer).
- *Example: We are a happy family.*

Define your first objective.

- Some people say you only want to have one objective so you are really focused, let's agree to not have more than three.
- Objectives are the destination. They answer the question: "Where do you want to go?". They are ambitious, qualitative, aspirational and inspirational. They are expressed in the present tense as if it was already done.
- *Example: We host a wonderful barbecue party.*

Identify who are the people involved that could make or break success.

- *Example: Guests, family, we can even distinguish some of the guests and family saying that we will have children or teenagers. One actor or stakeholder that could break success: Mosquitoes.*

Identify the behavior you want the people involved to adopt so that you can achieve your objective.

- For each of the stakeholders, identify the most impactful behavioral changes that need to happen so you can achieve

your objective.
- *Example: You want the mosquitoes not to show up at the party, or if they show up you don't want them to bite anybody.*

Define Key Results that will quantify how you will reach your objective.

- Key Results are a way to measure that the behavioral change you want to get is really happening.
- *Example: A Key Result that measures that mosquitoes don't bite is: Nobody has been bitten by a mosquito during the party.*
- Key Results guide the action on a day to day basis. They need to be a stretch showing your ambition, difficult, not impossible, 70% should be a good reach.
- They are measurable and time-bound formulated like "increase or decrease an indicator from x to y by the end of a date."

Note that when you define Objectives and Key Results, you have to understand the why (the objective you want to achieve), the who (the people involved), the how (how their behavior should change so you can achieve your objective), but you can leave the what (what you will do to affect the behavioral change) for a later time.

- *In our example, the 'what' could be to provide mosquito repellent to all the guests. The 'what' are the deliverables, or the activities.*

One last thing. Remember that it took time for Sandrine and Joel to get to Objectives and Key Results that made sense for their team (like the one below). So don't expect to write them perfectly on your first attempt.

- Objective: Improve the maintainability of the product by reducing the complexity of its core components.
- As measured by:
- Key Result #1: No team members have less than half the reviews of another by the end of the quarter (so that we increase knowledge transfer in the team to continuously learn and develop from each other).
- Key Result #2: Less than 50 reviews provided by the team are considered meaningless or misleading by the end of the quarter.

Further Information

- Impact Mapping is the approach we used to identify the impact, the behavioral changes that need to happen so you can achieve success.
- For more information on Objectives and Key Results (OKRs), you can start with Wikipedia.

16

The Wheel of Life

What is it?

The Wheel of Life is a tool that helps you visualize how balanced and satisfactory your life is today.

Why use it?

You might tend to focus on specific areas of your life and forget or neglect other areas. The tool helps to visualize the current situation and creates the desire to improve in the areas that really matters to you.

Steps

First, pick 8 categories which to represent the important facets of your life. Ideas of categories are below:

- Health

- Relationships
- Social
- Cultural
- Career
- Business
- Financial
- Spiritual
- Personal growth
- Fun and Leisure
- Significant other
- Contribution
- *You could also decide to focus exclusively your wheel on the professional aspect of your life and identify only categories in that area.*

Use the area to label each piece of the pie chart below,

Rank how you are currently doing in each area from 0 to 10 like in the example below.

Reflect on how smooth or bumpy the wheel would roll if it were real.

Identify one action that would make improvements in one important area for you.

Come back to your wheel when you are ready for the next action.

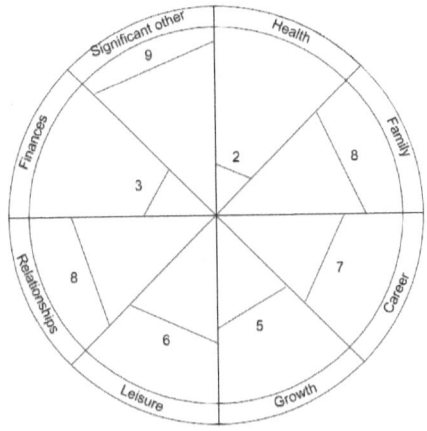

Example

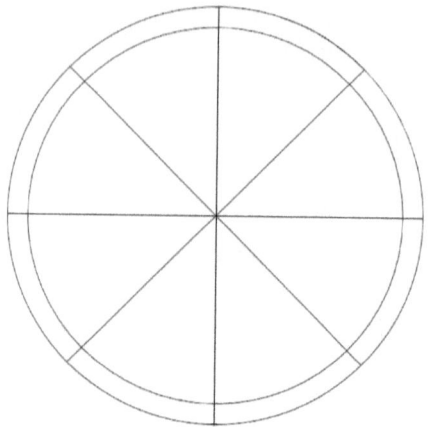

Template

Further Information

- Paul J. Meyer is the original creator of The Wheel of Life in the 1960s.

17

The Matrix of Principles

What is it?

The Matrix of Principles is a reflection tool to capture how team members understand Deming's 14 Management Principles.

Why use it?

Reflecting on the management principles enables the team to share their beliefs on management, to share their views on where the organization is, and to identify areas for improvement.

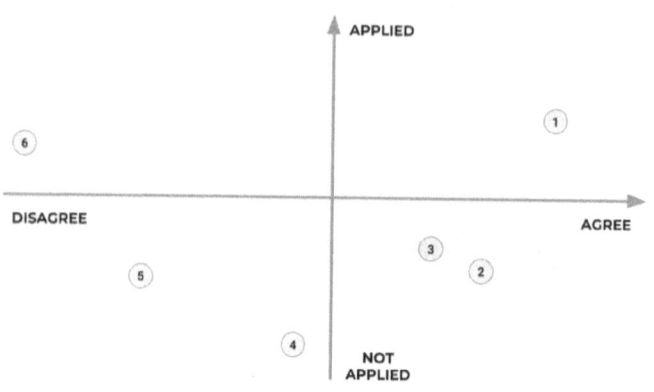

Steps

- Take a blank sheet of paper, or use a whiteboard,
- Draw a 2x2 matrix,
- The horizontal axis represents your agreement with the principle. On the right, you agree; on the left, you disagree,
- The vertical axis represents how the principle is applied to your organization. "Applied" at the top, "not applied" at the bottom,
- You will now position Deming's 14 Management Principles by placing their numbers on the matrix. Each team member uses a different color.
- After placing each principle, the facilitator asks the outliers to explain their position.
- The facilitator asks the group what ideas it inspires for the team.

You can use the tool for self-reflection. As a facilitator, it is useful to try the exercise first by yourself to be able to pick the principles that will most resonate with your team.

You can also use the Matrix of Principles with other principles. The ones from the Agile Manifesto are other principles that are great conversation starters.

Further Information

- Deming's 14 Management Principles
- Principles of the Agile Manifesto

This practice was first published in Changing Your Team From The Inside.

18

One-on-one

What is it?

A one-on-one is an approach to prepare and drive effective meetings with people you are not familiar with.

Why use it?

Creating a relationship with people is key to be able to work with them effectively.

Steps

Prepare a board that will make the agenda for the meeting visible:

Take a piece of paper (Letter or A4 will work)

Draw two lines to create 3 columns on the same width

Write on three mini sticky notes the three headings to give the meeting structure:

- To Do
- In Progress
- Done

Write the topics that will be covered during the meeting, one topic per mini sticky notes:

- Ice Breaker
- Professional Background
- Experience of ...
- 3 Wishes
- ???

The meeting starts with all the sticky notes in the "To Do" column (see the figure below).

Ice Breaker. The Ice Breaker is a game in which you take turns asking each other questions.

- Move the sticky note to "In Progress".
- You only have three questions each, and each person has the right to pass. Here are three examples:
- *If you could do anything in the entire world other than your current job, what would it be?*
- *What do you spend most of your spare time doing?*
- *What's your favorite holiday destination?*
- Once the Ice Breaker is Done, move the card to the "Done" column.

Professional background. You will now share your work history that led to your current role.

- Pick the next note in the "To Do" column and move it to "In Progress".
- You will start first, so make sure to be prepared to cover all your professional background in the minimum time.
- The other person will go next, once she is done, encourage her to move the card to done.

Experience of …

- Depending on Alexis' role, he has used notes on different topics. He used "Agile Experience" for a mission to drive a change toward agile approaches, "Management Experience" with a new manager, "Web Experience" while onboarding a new developer for a Web agency. Pick something that will be relevant to you in your context.

3 Wishes.

- Time for the 3 Wishes. You end with another game, asking a question: "If you could have three wishes for transforming your daily work and/or workplace, what would they be?" Once again, what the people say here will teach you a lot about the organization and their current mindset.

???

- The last note, with the three question marks, is a wild card to allow the other person to propose any additional topics to discuss. People will sometimes have nothing more to say, and sometimes they will suggest a topic that could be useful to cover in another meeting, not necessarily this one.

To Do	In Progress	Done
Ice-breaker		
Professional Background		
Agile Experience		
3 Wishes		
???		

Further Information

- Portia Tung proposed this one on one structure in her book The Dream Team Nightmare.
- The One-on-one experiment is the activity proposed in the Chapter 5 of Changing Your team From The Inside.

What do people say about it?

"I used it once again today, for the onboarding of a new collaborator who had just joined the team... I tell you only that after 40 minutes we were already like two best friends! Really powerful this workshop!" – Mario Esposito

19

How-to I work

What is it?

How-to I work is a practice meant for you to define the how-to describing the way you work and provide it to your coworker.

Why use it?

Your co-workers' feedback can help you learn what you have to adjust in your way of working. Another positive consequence is when your colleagues decide to work on their own "how-tos" it can become the foundation for the team to work on a *Team Agreement*.

Steps

The steps are meant to answer one question: How do I behave? By answering that question people know what to expect from you.

What is my typical day?

- When do you start your day?
- When do you end your day?
- If you work in an office, how do you commute? (It can help people to know that you could show up late, because of a problem on a train line.)
- Are there time periods during which you don't want to be interrupted? How do you signal that?

How do you recharge or take a break?

- Do you break for lunch?
- What is your favorite snack?

How do you communicate?

- Answering this question help people know how you prefer to use the different communication tools, for example, Alexis would say:
- *Urgent: Text me and then call me so I know I have to take your call*
- *Simple question or want to share something: Chat (whatever instant messaging system you use: irc, Slack, WhatsApp...*
- *Meeting: Video conference*
- *Update on the work we are doing: Through our tracking tool*
- *Public service announcement: Email*

How do you collaborate?

- For example:

- *Through shared documents on which people can comment and suggest, I dislike long email threads to discuss a topic and will probably be the one making the extra effort to move the discussion to a shared document.*
- *I love pair programming or even mob programming.*

In addition to that some people are very creative and add information like:

- One word that best describes how I work
- Background
- Responsibilities
- Tools
- Goals
- Workspace setup
- Favorite shortcut or hack
- Favorite side project

Further Information

- What is a "How-to"? Wikipedia has an answer for you.

20

The Four Agreements

What is it?

The Four Agreements is a practice to uncover the power of your words and your thoughts on yourself and others.

The Four Agreements were created by Don Miguel Ruiz:

1. **Be impeccable with your word.** "Speak with integrity. Say only what you mean. Avoid using the word to speak against yourself or to gossip about others. Use the power of your word in the direction of truth and love."
2. **Don't make assumptions.** "Find the courage to ask questions and to express what you really want. Communicate with others as clearly as you can to avoid misunderstandings, sadness and drama. With just this one agreement, you can completely transform your life."
3. **Don't take anything personally.** "Nothing others do is because of you. What others say and do is a projection of

their own reality, their own dream. When you are immune to the opinions and actions of others, you won't be the victim of needless suffering."

4. **Always do your best.** "Your best is going to change from moment to moment; it will be different when you are healthy as opposed to sick. Under any circumstances, simply do your best, and you will avoid self-judgment, self-abuse and regret."

Why use it?

Changing the way you speak or the way you think is not difficult but you need to invest a deliberate amount of energy to make it happen. Once you catch yourself with one of your automatic reactions, you can choose to change the way you express yourself to a new way.

Steps

Create a calendar for the next five days with two checkboxes for each day, one for the morning, one for the evening. Once you complete a session, check the box. Display the calendar where it is visible to you, Alexis keeps his on his desk; Michael prefers to have it next to his bed. You may also want to set reminders on your phone so that you really don't forget about the activity.

On day one, choose the agreement on which you will work during the next five days.

Morning:

- Choose an event or part of the day when you are going to be conscious of being impeccable with your words. It could be during a meeting, a casual conversation, or choosing to react differently when someone starts venting or gossiping.
- Tick the box on your calendar.

Evening:

- Reflect on the day and make a note on:
- How well you felt you did (this could be on a 1 to 5 scale or use green, yellow, red).
- What you could do differently tomorrow.
- Tick the box on your calendar.

At the end of the fifth day:

- Look back at your notes on the past five days and evaluate your ratings.
- What do you notice?
- What conversations are more difficult than others?
- Go back to day one and begin again with another agreement.

Remember, rewiring the brain takes repetition, so it's better to focus on changing one automatic reaction at a time.

Don't be disappointed if you fail. It is a little bit like meditation and a wandering mind. Minds wander. That's what minds do. Meditation is a practice that trains you to notice that the mind is wandering and to bring it back to the practice.

Further Information

- The Toltec Agreements, Don Miguel Ruiz (Wikipedia)
- The Four Agreements: A Practical Guide to Personal Freedom, Don Miguel Ruiz.

21

Delegation Poker

What is it?

Delegation Poker is an activity for a team to clarify the responsibilities of team members and stakeholders.

Each card of the deck represent one level of delegation among the seven available:

1. Tell: I will tell them.
2. Sell: I will try and sell it to them.
3. Consult: I will consult and then decide.
4. Agree: We will agree together.
5. Advise: I will advise but they decide.
6. Inquire: I will inquire after they decide.
7. Delegate: I will fully delegate.

Why use it?

The objective of Delegation Poker is to collaboratively define how the team delegates decisions and tasks.

Steps

You first need to download the cards and print them. Follow the link in the reference to find the cards. You can also play the delegation poker online. All the players have all the levels of delegation in hand.

Brainstorm a short list of scenarios on which a delegation decision have to be made.

Examples of scenario could be:

- *Hire a new team member*
- *Purchase new equipment*
- *Travel to a conference*
- *...*
- *Once you have a first list of scenario, you are ready for the second step.*

Pick the first scenario.

Each player chooses the level of delegation that is required for the scenario.

All the players show their cards at the same time (so that they don't influence each other).

The players with the lowest card, and the highest card explain the reason of their choice.

Once an agreement is reached, you can capture it in a delegation board.

You don't need to count the points, as the game is more about starting the conversation and agreeing on how the team will behave.

Further Information

- Delegation Poker and Delegation Board, Management 3.0 Practices.
- Delegation Poker online, Troy Daniel.

22

Team Agreements

What is it?

Team Agreements is a practice that results in a document that formalizes how each individual agrees to work as a member of a team.

Why use it?

Team Agreements are critical to the success of a team. By writing your team agreements, you define your standard. You set the baseline that you will improve in the future.

Furthermore, getting to team agreements is a collaborative effort for the team. It is a good first step to increase collaboration.

Steps

Depending on if you are a co-located team or a distributed team, your team agreements can be formalized as a shared electronic document, or as a simple sheet of flipboard paper which is signed by each team member, and displayed on one wall of their workspace.

The steps to get there have to be collaborative. A practice Alexis likes is to review the team agreements at the end of each team retrospective.

In the team agreements, you answer the question: How do we behave?

What aspects do you want to cover in your team agreements?

- Quick brainstorm on all the aspects you want to cover like information, communication...
- Then you will answer your own questions for each aspect, take what follows as example you can use to build your first team agreements.

How does the team handle information?

- What kind of information do we need to achieve our work?
- How do we share the information inside and outside of the team?
- How do we know what everybody is doing?

How does the team communicate

- What are the tools the team uses to communicate?
- Phone or video conference: why do we prefer phone calls or video conferences for some conversations?
- Instant messaging: for what kind of message, what time of the day...
- Email: do we use emails inside the team or do we communicate using the tool we use to track our work?
- When do we want not to be interrupted? How do we signal that to others? How do we handle external interruptions? Do we nominate an interruption handler?

How do we collaborate?

- How do we produce documents, code...
- When do we use pair programming or mob programming?
- Why do we have meetings? What are their purposes?
- How do we behave in meetings? How do we handle devices? How strict are we on time? On attendance?

How do we provide or receive feedback?

- Do we have a specific time, setup, tools... to provide or receive feedback?

How do we handle conflict?

How do we manage performance?

How do we hire new team members?

The list of questions could be infinite. So the best practice is to start small and review your agreements regularly. This is a place for the team to experiment with various approaches and to improve.

Further Information

- The Social Contract, shared on the Open Practice Library.

23

Retrospective

What is it?

A Retrospective is a specific meeting in which a team reflects on what happened during a period of time (one iteration, one week, one month, one quarter...).

A classic retrospective follows a five stage structure:

- Set the stage: So people agree that regardless of what they discover, they understand and believe that everyone did the best job they could (paraphrasing Norm Kerth's prime directive).
- Gather data: To make visible and factual the obvious. We don't have the same experience of reality. We don't remember the same things. We are not affected by things and events the same way.
- Generate insights: By taking a step back and observe and discuss the data the team gathered.

- Decide what to do: To define one or two actions the team will take after the retrospective.
- Close the retrospective: To get people to reflect on the time invested to decide for improvement actions.

Why use it?

The structured reflection leads the team to make decisions, either to reinforce positive behaviors, or to invest time to improve their way of working.

Steps

Your experiment is to facilitate a retrospective for your team. Get the buy-in from relevant stakeholders is your first challenge, and then:

- Select a period of time that the team will reflect on.
- Select a retrospective format on the Retrospective Techniques board (If you don't know, pick the Timeline Retrospective).
- Prepare the retrospective by doing a simulation by yourself so you get a first feel of how it works.
- Prepare the logistics (meeting room, office supplies, calendar invites...)
- Plan time for you before the meeting so you can be in a good mindset to facilitate the retrospective (you may want to find someone external to the team to facilitate your first one?)
- And just do it.
- And then of course, reflect on what happen with your own

retrospective of the retrospective.

Further Information

- Retrospective Techniques board, by Philip Rogers
- Agile Retrospective, by Esther Derby and Diana Larsen
- Prime Directive, by Norm Kerth

24

Pomodoro

What is it?

Pomodoro is an approach to manage time and keep focus on the most important things. A Pomodoro represents 25 minutes of work without any interruption.

Why use it?

Context switching costs a lot of time and energy. Interruptions force you to leave your current train of thought and switch context. Surprisingly, people are keen to blame others when they are interrupted but don't seem to care as much when the source of their interruptions is themselves and their way of working. The Pomodoro Technique is a simple and efficient way of solving that.

Steps

Pomodoro is a five-step process:

- Plan the tasks to do at the beginning of the day and sequence them in order of importance.
- Stick to the list during the day for each Pomodoro cycle.
- Record your daily observations.
- Convert the raw data to information.
- Visualize daily information to find improvement areas.

During the day your daily work is organized in Pomodoros. During a Pomodoro, no interruptions are allowed, no phone, no notification, no mail... Except if your Pomodoro is about dealing with your emails.

Pick the first task and start the 25 minute Pomodoro timer. After 25 minutes, take a 5 minute break... The first time, your might find the time goes quickly, yet at the same time, it's a terrific opportunity to adjust your posture, breath, drink a glass of water... From time to time, the temptation to continue to work even if the timer rings is high, so there is some Pomodoro software that can block the keyboard if you need it.

After 4 Pomodoros, the break is longer from 15 to 30 minutes. This can seem long. Alexis tried to reduce this time to 10 minutes but observed that he was not taking enough breaks before feeling "too" tired or "too" stretched.

Either for a short or long break, it can be difficult to stop and to stop to think about the work you are doing. Alexis has also observed that when he can do it, it's straightforward to get back to the previous activity after the break.

At the end of each Pomodoro, you add a tick to the current task. You can also capture other information, like how you feel about the task (Alexis uses smileys). In doing so, you will be able to capture how many Pomodoros you use for each of your tasks. It will help you in the reflection phase to identify improvement areas.

Further Information

- The Pomodoro Technique
- Of course it is on Wikipedia

25

Personal Management System

What is it?

The *Personal Management System* is a way of managing your flow of work from ideas to completion. The system is a combination of the Getting Things Done workflow managed via a Kanban board.

Why use it?

People tend to have between no system at all, or minimalist systems like to-do lists. The to-do lists have a tendency to become infinite overwhelming lists. Furthermore, the longer they are, the harder it is to choose what is important to do now. The Personal Management System supports your decisions about what's coming next in an efficient way.

Steps

The Getting Things Done workflow has four main steps:

Capture: Capture ideas, requests, tasks in the Inbox column.

Clarify: Every day, review the Inbox column and clarify the cards that are in it by asking those questions:

Is it actionable?

NO, choose between:

- *Trash: not a good idea to invest energy on it.*
- *Someday/Maybe: it is not no, but definitely not now.*
- *Reference: could be useful in the future.*

YES, is it a single step to complete?

- NO, move the card in the column *Project*
- YES, is it more than 2 minutes?
- *NO: Do it now.*
- *YES: Move to the Hold Column.*

Organize:

Review the cards in the *In Progress* column:

- Do you have time scheduled to work on the task?
- *NO: Schedule it.*
- *YES: Good, next task.*

Once you are done with the In Progress column review the cards in the To Do This Week column.

- Do you have time scheduled to work on the task?
- *NO: Schedule it. If you see that you don't have available time to schedule a task in your week, you have to make the decision to move the card back to the Hold column.*
- *YES: Good, next task.*

Reflect:

At least once a week (Alexis loves to do it on Friday), reflect how it went during the week:

- Have the things that matter been done?
- What are the specific struggles?
- What could you adjust in your way of working?

Review the cards in the *Hold* column as it may be the time to select them for next week.

Review the cards in the *Project* column to define what is the first step to take to make progress on a project, create a card for the next step and move it to the appropriate column.

Review the cards in the Someday/Maybe column, some may be ready to act upon, some may be ready for the trash.

A Kanban board is used to manage the whole workflow. Here is a description of the board starting with the first column:

- Inbox: All ideas, requests, tasks arrive in the Inbox column
- Someday/Maybe
- Project
- Hold
- To Do This Week
- In Progress
- Done
- Reference

Further Information

- Kanban board
- Getting Things Done (GTD)

About the Authors

Alexis Monville

Hi, I'm Alexis, a member of the Engineering Leadership Team at Enterprise Open Source Software company Red Hat.

For more than 20 years, I have used and built software in diverse sectors such as the automotive industry, a dot-com startup, IT consulting, public sector, software development, and my management and organization consulting and coaching firm.

From 2011 until Red Hat acquired eNovance in 2014, I nurtured and grew the eNovance agile organization from a few individuals to more than a hundred people. During this time, I maintained the team's focus on delivering private cloud services with OpenStack while building an open and people-centric culture.

I regularly speak about management and agile transformation and participate in industry events such as the Open Infrastructure Summit, Open World Forum, and Agile Lean Europe.

I love coaching and mentoring software engineers. It is the foundation to builds high impact sustainable organizations.

I am the author of Changing Your Team From The Inside, a book published in 2018. With the second book, I am a Software Engineer and I am in Charge, Michael and I want to help increase your impact and satisfaction at work.

Michael Doyle

Hi, I'm Michael, a Conversion Copywriter and a Software Engineering Leadership Coach.

For more than 15 years I've worked shoulder-to-shoulder with software engineers from around the globe.

In organizations from medical devices and mobile media to wide area networking and enterprise open source, I've experienced how developing yourself as a next generation leader in software engineering can be filled with ambiguity. You're not sure which actions are the right actions, and you don't want to fail.

My solution is simple, Fear + Action = Courage.

As a leadership coach, I ask questions that draw out your vision and strengths. From your new vantage point you will see the actions you need to take, giving you courage to propel yourself to the next level of your career.

As a recent client put it, "Working with Michael was like being hit by a tsunami of insight."

Working with Alexis, and combining my copywriting and coaching skills, I've now been able to package this leadership development experience into this book.

I am a Software Engineer and I am in Charge is a practical approach to increasing your impact and satisfaction at work.